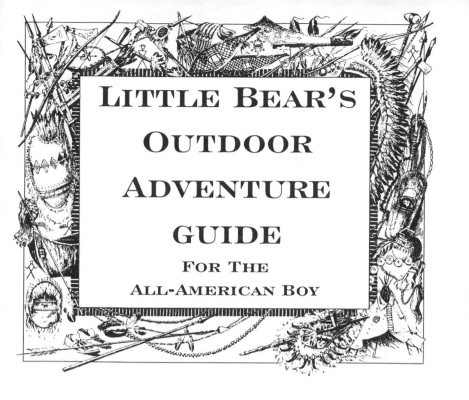

LITTLE BEAR'S OUTDOOR ADVENTURE GUIDE

FOR THE ALL-AMERICAN BOY

BY
RICHARD "LITTLE BEAR" WHEELER
PROFUSELY ILLUSTRATED
PUBLISHED 2000 AD

D0094652

Published By
Mantle Ministries: 228 Still Ridge
Bulverde, Texas 78163
http://www.mantlemin.com or e-mail mantleministries@cs.com

INTRODUCTION

Over the years as I have traveled throughout the U.S. as an evangelist and ministered dressed in various buckskins and furs of all sorts, I have had countless parents tell me that they have children who are "just like you, Little Bear." Since I am dressed somewhat like a pioneer, many parents tell me that their children get the urge to pick up road kill animals to skin and tan them. These parents, after being begged so much, work up enough nerve to come up and ask me if it is possible to skin road kill critters and tan them. The answer I always give them is most certainly yes. The next question is how?

I knew how they feel, because as a boy I dreamed of being a trapper myself but was frustrated that beavers were all gone from the streets of Los Angeles, California. I began to look around, and, lo and behold, I spotted pocket gophers free for the trapping. I had a trapping line down my street and would trap, skin, and tan those rodents, much to the joy of the little old ladies who had vegetable gardens in their back yards. When I was a little older, I rode my bike to the Santa Monica canyons and went for "big game" such as raccoons and rabbits. Those days I spent trapping kept me innocent and saved me from bad friends, sex, and drugs. They were clean, healthy adventures that many youth still long for. May this book inspire all those frustrated would-be modern pioneer boys and girls who want to relive some of America's primitive past.

I have collected from my personal library various out-of-print trapping and tanning books. With the information compiled in this book you will be able to skin, sell, tan, and perhaps even cook the meat. Those of you who have a touch of Jedediah Smith blood in their veins will learn the skills necessary to become a general outdoorsman or woman.

I

There is very little need for home tanning for the average citizen today. With the development of modern equipment for commercial tanning and the manufacturing of various alternative materials, people simply wear the leather goods manufactured by others. There has also come to be a stigma connected with the killing of animals by the animal rights movement. The trapper today is looked upon as some sort of evil monster who kills innocent animals for the sheer pleasure of killing. This is far from the truth for the trapper who sells pelts as a livelihood and for the student who traps for personal use.

The first simple form of tanning of furs was called "rub tanning." Rub tanning is done by grasping the dried hide in two hands and rubbing the flesh side together until the skin becomes pliable and soft. Many Eskimos, among other non-commercial tanners, still use this method today.

"Chew tanning," also developed by various ancient people, consisted of chewing the dried hides and pulling at the same time. Over a period of chewing time, the hide was softened. You may wonder why in the world chew tanning ever developed. One of the reasons, in my opinion, was that during the bitter cold winter months, when chores like tanning had to be done indoors, there was limited room to use tanning tools to stretch, scrape, and work the hides. Using the teeth was a method that took only as much space as the tanner himself took up. Alaskan Eskimos and Indians still use both "rub" and "chew" tanning today. It was the practice of many tribes even to urinate on the hides as part of the tanning process because the acid in the urine would aid in breaking the tough leather fibers.

Tanning also involved soaking hides in water with oak bark, sumac, hemlock, and other barks, woods, and weeds that contained tannic acid. Soaking the hides in bark would dye the hide and add color to the natural cream-colored hide.

II

The Great Plains Indians, such as the Sioux, used the brains of animals and human urine to do most of their tanning. There is a rule of thumb that says, "Every animal has enough brains to tan his own hide." If the Indians of the Great Plains desired to remove the hair from hides, they soaked the hides in a thick solution of water and wood ashes. These methods are called "Indian tanning." "Indian tanning" leaves the leather with no smooth surface on either side. Both sides of the leather are "suede" or rough-feeling leather. You can readily tell if moccasins or garments are really Indian-made by just looking at the leather. Indian leather was fairly rough and uncivilized looking. Today's leather is fine, soft, and pliable; this is due to the use of machines that work the leather.

Today tanners soak skins in a saturated solution of water and lime to remove the hair. Hand tanning is tedious, and the results are not as good as commercially tanned leather. However, many people continue to hand tan at home because of the sheer pleasure and because of the tremendous savings of money compared to buying commercially prepared leather.

Midwestern Indians oil tanned furs. The skins were soaked in water, then wrung out. Fish or bear oil was rubbed and pounded into the soft skins to replace the water. When the skins were saturated with oil, they were heated over a small, controlled fire. The Indians built a mini-tepee over the fire with tree limbs and slung the hide over these poles. The smoke was thus allowed to filter upward and saturate the hide. The oil decomposed under the heat, leaving the skins tanned.

We are indebted to those men who have taken the time to record the various tanning methods for the benefit of future generations. Men such as George Herter, Raymond Thompson, Deep-River Jim, and A. R. Harding are some of those pioneers, all long gone from the fields of fur and fun.

III

Following are some tanning methods from years gone by.

Alum tanning is another old tanning process. However, it was a very poor one and not worth trying today.

Chrome tanning, or the use of chrome salts for tanning, began at the end of the 19th century. It is widely used for shoe leathers. I personally do not like this method because of the unnatural chemical color it leaves on the hides.

The tanning of furs is completely different from the tanning of leathers. To the best of my knowledge, this book is the only complete source for this information. Fur tanners for centuries have kept their methods entirely secret. The methods described here for tanning furs are the exact methods used by the world's finest custom fur tanners. Using these methods you can get perfect results. The furs you tan in your home will be tanned as well as or better than any tanned by any other method in the entire world.

All furs are worth far more when tanned than untanned. You can sell your tanned furs or make them into garments and sell them. Either way, you will be able to command three to four times the price you would gain by selling the furs untanned.

One further word: Because most of the sources used in this book were originally printed in the late 1800s and early 1900s, the types of equipment mentioned may now be called by different names and in many cases are manufactured by different companies today. Therefore, at the end of this book, I have provided a reference list to help in locating equipment and supplies. Also check your local hardware store or trapping goods store for current equipment.

Richard "Little Bear" Wheeler

CONTENTS.

ALL ABOUT TANNING

CARE OF FUR PELTS OR SKINS

Obtaining hides is the easiest part of the entire process of skinning and tanning. Several steps must be taken immediately in order to assure yourself of a useful hide. Following is an outline of these basic steps for tanning. They are further described in detail throughout this book.

1. Wash
2. Flesh
3. Wash
4. Rinse
5. Tan
6. Neutralize
7. Rinse
8. Stretch
9. Lubricate
10. Dry and soften

It is absolutely essential that the fur skin reaches the tanning vat without any damage to the hair. The hair is the valuable part and must be carefully protected. The fur of "road kill" is usually too damaged to preserve: however, the pelt can still be used for hairless leather. Fur skins require far greater attention to tan than hides that are to be used just for leather without any hair on the hide.

Furry animals should be skinned as soon as possible after death and while warm to avoid hair slipping during the tanning process. If the animal is frozen, it must be thawed slowly. Do not thaw the animal rapidly by placing it near a stove or any other source of heat. This will cause hair to come off, resulting in a hairless pelt, usable for leather only.

Skinning an animal cased is the best method, as it does the least damage to the fur. Some animals, like beaver, bear, and seal, are customarily skinned open. Casing is skinning the animal in such a way that the legs are left in the round. The best way to understand this would be to picture wearing a glove and instead of slipping it off in the usual way, pulling it inside out. Casing is pulling the hide from the animal inside out.

Beaver and seal would actually be better if skinned cased. Bears are usually made into rugs, and skinning them open is most practical for this use.

Use a sharp knife for skinning. I prefer a fisherman's knife, which can be purchased inexpensively at a sporting goods store. I highly recommend skinning gloves, also sold at most sporting goods stores, to prevent cuts to the hands.

By hand pull the skin from the hide as much as possible. Use the knife to cut the muscles and tissues just under the skin. In skinning animals such as mink, marten, and fox, carefully scrape out the tissues under the toe pads and toes, leaving on the pads and claws. This can be done with a used razor blade or small, very sharp knife. The skins then can be made into hats or shoulder capes.

The hides of muskrats are very tender, and great care must be used to keep them from tearing. The hide of a squirrel is extremely tough and difficult to pull off from the legs, body, and head. On all animals the muscles and flesh only thinly covers the belly areas. Use care not to cut through or tear these thin areas, or the organs will fall out, making a real mess of an otherwise fairly simple job.

FUR BEARING ANIMALS
SKINNED "CASED"

Muskrat, mink, otter, fox, coyote, squirrel, raccoon, opossum, skunk, weasel, wolf, and wolverine are always skinned cased (as illustrated in Figure 1), if they are to be sold to a commercial tannery. Beaver skins are traditionally stretched round. All other open skinned pelts are stretched to their natural shape. If you do not want to sell the hides, but only tan them, you will not need to case the hides.

Start cutting just above the hind leg pads and cut to the tail then to the other hind leg pad. Skin out the paws with the pads and claws left on. This makes the hides of the animals look better, and they will be worth more money, if you plan to sell them. On animals like the muskrat, skinning out the paws is not required. Just cut around the paws or cut off the paws.

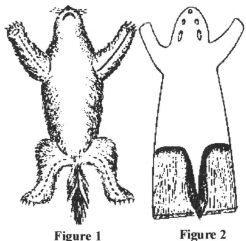

Figure 1   Figure 2

**Fur stretching, fur side out
and fur side in**

With a very sharp knife or razor blade slit the tail completely to the tip and remove the tailbone (except in the case of muskrats, whose tail has no valuable fur on it). Now carefully, by hand, pull and cut the skin carefully and slowly from the feet toward the animal's head. In the case of small animals pull the skin off the front legs and skin out the paws. For muskrats just cut off the paws. In the case of large animals, with a sharp knife make cuts on the inside of the

3

front legs and work off the skin. Be careful to cut around the eyes, ears, nose, and jaws. Start the cuts at the edge of the eyes and ears. Skin the gristle (cartilage material) out of the ears carefully if the pelt is to be used for a scarf or for mounting. If the gristle is left in the ears, the hair often comes off the ears in the tanning process.

Three things cause untanned furs to hair-slip or rot: moisture, warm temperatures, and excess fat left on the skin. Fresh, wet, warm skin invites bacteria to grow rapidly and destroy the skin and hair. Immediately after skinning, the hide must be stretched and dried or frozen to prevent damage from bacteria.

Freezing for too long is bad for pelts, too, as skin can develop frostbite areas. If for some reason the hair slips, do not get discouraged; you can always proceed with the tanning and use the finished hairless pelt as leather for various items such as shoes, bags, belts, and leather laces.

With a dull knife or spoon remove as much fat, flesh, and muscles as possible from the hide. Then put the pelt onto a drying stretcher, fur side in, as shown in Figure 2. Figure 3 shows patterns for wooden frames to case hides.

Let the hide partially dry; then reverse the hide and put the hide back onto the stretcher fur side out. Let dry. Unless you dry the hide both fur side out and fur side in, the buyer will not be able to see the value of the hair. The muskrat is the only furbearer that should be completely dried fur side in. When a hide is put onto a fur stretcher, the pelt must be stretched and held down, usually with tacks. Use a dull knife or spoon to remove more fat and muscle pieces after the hide is on the stretcher. As soon as the pelts are dry, remove them from the stretchers.

Another type of stretcher is the stretch-and-lace, shown in Figure 4. The Indians often used this method.

One other simple way of stretching is to stretch the hide while fresh off the animal onto a plywood sheet using a heavy-duty stapler, and staple as you shape the hide. Salt the hide once the hide is stretched with hair down and flesh side up. Allow to dry up to three weeks. Salt can then be removed and the hide stored.

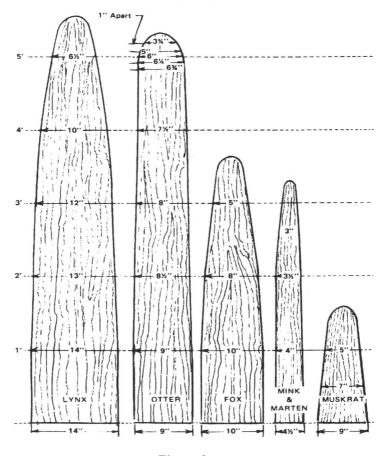

Figure 3

Plywood frames for casing. Pelts are stretched by nailing to the frame, hair side down and the skin pulled up to the head of the nails to allow air to circulate in the hair and under the skin.

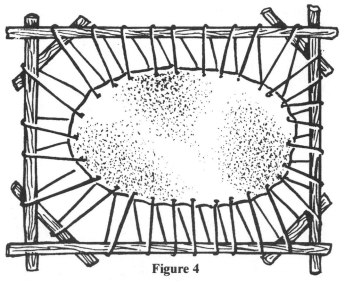

Figure 4
Stretch-and-Lace Method

SALTING THE HIDES

If you will not be tanning the pelts right away, you will need to salt them. Salt acts as a preservative to keep the hide from rotting before the tanning process. If you choose to skin the hide off the animal and tan all in the same day, you can skip the salting process. Store the pelts in a dry place free from bugs, rodents, and moths until time to tan them. You could also seal them in a plastic bag.

Bear skins can be nailed to the inside wall of an old building to dry. Do not nail them to an outside wall, because the sun may dry them too rapidly and spoil them. Great care must be used to remove all fat from the bear skin before and after stretching. Salt hides after fat is removed and allow to dry up to three weeks. Salt can then be removed with a brush or a dull putty knife, and the hide can be stored.

On large skins such as bear, the use of clean salt on the flesh side of the skin will pull the moisture out of the skin much more quickly than natural drying. To apply salt, stretch the skin out flat, flesh side up. Cover the skin with about one-eighth inch of salt. A general guideline for the amount of salt to use is a pound of salt for each pound of the pelt. Fine salt is by far the best to use, but rock salt, or ice cream salt, can be used. After the salt has been on the skin for three days, remove the salt. Leave the skin in a cool, dry place until completely dry. Do not put the skin in the sun or near a stove. When the skin is dry remove the skin from the plywood. Store in a cool, dry place, free from moths and mice.

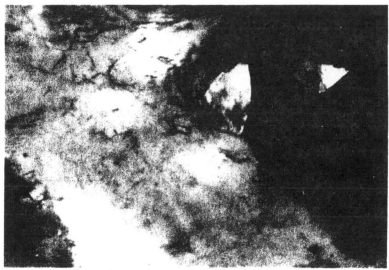

Figure 5

It is important to scrape most fat, and salt hide down if not tanning immediately.

Salting sets the hair much better than air drying, preventing any shedding of the hair. Salting helps prevent the fibers of the skin from sticking together during drying. A salt-cured hide will not crack or break as easily as does an unsalted, air-dried pelt. Salting is desirable for any skin that is to be tanned with the hair on.

7

If a pelt is to be tanned soon after skinning, rinse the skin in cool water to remove blood stains. Flesh the pelt carefully. (That is, scrape off flesh, fat, and muscle.) Wash with a detergent in lukewarm water to remove all fat and oils. Rinse in clear water; then put the pelt in the tanning vat.

PROFESSIONAL TANNING
WITH ACID

A top-quality tanned pelt depends on a number of factors, each factor depending upon the others. Some of these factors include the time of year the animal is harvested, the health and diet of the animal, the proper skinning and fleshing of the skin before tanning, the strength and temperature of the tanning solution, and the amount of time spent "breaking," or softening, the pelt after it is tanned. Usually the colder the weather, the better the pelt. The pelt must be prime to be worth top value. The skin of a prime pelt is usually quite white. An unprime pelt is usually quite blue or gray.

A well tanned pelt is produced in three major steps. The first step is to flesh the pelt, or remove all the unwanted matter such as muscle, flesh, fat, blood, and dirt. The pelt skin should contain just the protein fibers that make up the skin and the hair. The second step is to treat these skin protein fibers with a tanning solution that will stabilize their structure. The third step is to work the tanned skin fibers until they are soft and can be used in a garment or other product.

HOW TO SOFTEN A DRIED PELT OR SKIN FOR TANNING

Make a softening solution in a large container. The container that holds the softening solution must be large enough to hold all of the skins that you are going to work and still have plenty of room to work the skins up and down during the softening process.

Use the following formula to make the solution:

1/4 cup of salt

1 ounce of borax (a common brand is Boraxo™, found at grocery or drugstores)

2 ounces of strong detergent per gallon of cool, clean water

Soak the skins in this solution to bring them back to much the same soft, flexible condition that they were in when you skinned them from the animal. Soak the pelts only long enough to soften the skin or hide. If you soak them too long, the water will cause the hair to slip and come off the skin. Small skins can be worked with your hands during the soaking to speed up the soaking process. The time that it takes to soften a pelt depends on the condition and the thickness of the skin. A thin skin, such as a muskrat or fox, will soften up well in an hour or two. A large beaver pelt will take eight to ten hours to soften properly.

FLESHING THE SKIN

Although you have already fleshed the skin when you removed it from the animal and also when you put it on the stretcher to dry, bits of flesh, muscle, and fat may remain which will show up on the soaked skin. Use a stiff wire brush, a sharp, fine-toothed metal scraper, or the back

9

edge of a large knife to scrape off this excess. Also, a six-inch piece of steel pipe about one inch in diameter with a wooden handle forced in one end and the other end sharpened from the inside works well.

Fleshing can be done with the skin stretched out on a flat piece of board or plywood or on a fleshing beam. See Figure 6. Care must be taken to avoid cutting the skin or exposing the hair roots, which can happen very easily when using any sharp tools.

Bear, beaver, raccoon, and seal skins are usually very fat and have to be treated by a special process. Wash such skins in kerosene. Gasoline should never be used, because it is extremely dangerous. A single static spark of electricity from the hair will cause gasoline to explode. Place the skins, damp from the cleaning solution and rinsing, in a plastic container with enough kerosene to soak them thoroughly. Work the skins until all fat is washed from the skin. This takes hand work as well as working with a wood plunger. For very heavy or very greasy skins, several such degreasings may be necessary. Then wash the skin in water and detergent to remove all traces of the kerosene.

WASHING PELTS WITH A DETERGENT

After the pelt is fleshed, wash it in clean water and a strong detergent. A stiff fiber brush can be used on the larger skins to remove all animal fat. A wire brush can be used on some skins. If the fat is not removed it will prevent the tanning solution from soaking into the skin. Also, any fat left in the skin may become rancid after tanning and smell bad.

A good method to wash beaver, raccoon, bear, and seal skins is to stretch them out on a piece of plywood. Sprinkle the skin generously with detergent. Sprinkle on a small amount of water. With a stiff fiber brush scrub the skins well.

RINSING PELTS

Rinse the pelts in cool, clean water at least two times or more. This must be done to remove all traces of the detergent. If the detergent is left in the skin it will weaken the tanning solution. After each rinse, the skin must be squeezed out, not twisted out.

The skin should now be very soft and free of fat, blood, extra loose flesh, and dirt. The pelt is now ready to place in tanning solution. Remember not to twist out water, but squeeze in order not to pull hair out while twisting.

TANNING VAT

When using the acid tanning method, do not use a metal container. Use a plastic garbage can or plastic bucket. Plastic garbage cans and buckets are inexpensive and satisfactory; metal is dangerous to use. It must be large enough to hold all of the skins that you have ready to tan. The garbage can or bucket must be clean. It should have a lid so small children and curious adults cannot get into it or poke into it.

The vat should be placed in a temperature around 65°-75°F. If the temperature gets higher than this, the acid may damage the skins. If the temperature gets colder than 65°F, the tanning will work but will go very slowly. The size of the container you use depends upon the kind and number of skins you tan. Twenty muskrat skins will fit nicely into a five-gallon plastic bucket. A good sized black bear hide will need a thirty-gallon container or vat.

THE TANNING SOLUTION

The tanning solution is made up of clean water, salt and sulphuric acid. The water is very important. The water must be clean and it is best to use soft water. Water with a high mineral content can cause undesirable results or not the very best results in tanning. If the water is high in iron, the acid and the iron may darken or blacken the skins. Rain water or melted snow water is the very best to use for the tanning solution.

The salt must be clean. Rock salt works well and is not as expensive as fine table salt, but it takes longer to dissolve than table salt.

The sulphuric acid can be one of three kinds. The first kind is concentrated sulphuric acid like that used in laboratories. The second is new battery fluid like that put in new batteries. Do not take the fluid out of a battery. Use only new battery fluid, as it comes out of the plastic bags. Sulphuric acid is most commonly known as car battery acid and can be secured at auto repair garages of most large car dealerships, or some auto parts stores. If going to a Sears Battery Shop, bring your own glass container, and ask a service person to give you a little for a project. He or she usually will not even charge you for it. Do not use a metal can to hold acid, as it will cause harmful fumes. The third form of sulphuric acid is sodium bisulfate. This is a crystal form and may be easier and safer to handle under some circumstances.

The amounts of each kind of acid to use for one gallon of water are as follows:

Choice 1
1 gallon of water
1 pound of salt
1 ounce of concentrated liquid sulphuric acid

Choice 2
1 gallon of water
1 pound of salt
4 ounces of new, unused battery fluid

Choice 3
1 gallon of water
1pound of salt
1/2 cup of sodium bisulfate crystals

In addition to these three kinds of acid, you can use oxalic acid. Oxalic acid is more expensive and, like sulphuric acid, is poisonous. Like all of the various sulphuric acids, oxalic acid cannot be sent by mail or air freighted where passengers are carried in a plane. Oxalic acid must be shipped by freight shipments only.

The mixture of oxalic acid is as follows:

1 gallon of water
1 pound of salt
2 ounces of oxalic acid

HOW TO MIX THE
ACID TANNING SOLUTION

Be sure that your plastic container is clean. Pour clean water that is around 70°F.

For each gallon of water, add one pound of table salt. Use a wooden stick to stir all the salt until completely dissolved. Using a plastic or glass **(never metal)** measuring cup, measure the amount of sulphuric acid and drip down the side of the tilted plastic container very slowly. Always add the acid to the water; never under any circumstances add the water to the acid. Even when you add the acid slowly, the acid will hiss and bubble and give off a strong odor. Do not breathe in the fumes of the acid that come from the mixing. Turn your head away from the fumes, and wear a filtered mask.

Now stir the entire mixture with a wooden stick. The acid is diluted enough so that you can put your hands into the tanning solution. It is a good idea to rinse the acid measuring cup out in the tanning solution.

CAUTION: When using sulphuric acid, be sure that no young children are around. Be sure that it is stored where children cannot find it. Mark it "POISON," along with the universal symbol of a skull and cross bones.

The tanning solution is now ready to be used. Put the pelts that are ready for the tanning solution into the vat. Be sure that all skins are completely covered by the tanning solution. You can use your hands, but if you keep your hands in the solution for a long time, the salt and sulphuric acid will cause your hands to become red and sore. It is always best to use rubber gloves to protect your hands.

HOW LONG TO LEAVE THE PELTS IN THE TANNING SOLUTION

The thicker the skin, the longer it takes to tan the skin. You should plan ahead and allow time to take the skins out on time. A light skin like a muskrat or a fox will tan in two or three days. A heavier skin like a beaver or raccoon may take four or five days. If necessary you can leave the pelts in the tanning solution for a much longer period of time than necessary. Up to thirty days will not hurt the pelts as long as the temperature stays below 75°F.

HOW LONG TO USE
THE SAME SOLUTION

The tanning solution can be used until it starts to smell bad. This depends on how clean the skins were when they were first put into the solution. The pieces of fat and flesh that come off from the skin in the tanning vat will gradually become rancid and smell bad in a few weeks at 70°F.

NEUTRALIZING THE TANNING
SOLUTION

After the pelts are removed from the tanning solution, they must be neutralized. The tanning solution contains sulphuric acid which, if not neutralized, will continue acting on the skin and eventually will weaken the skin fibers.

When you remove the pelts from the tanning solution, squeeze all possible solution out of them. Do not twist the skins; squeeze them.

To neutralize the tanned pelts, put them into a solution containing one ounce of borax per gallon of cool, clean water, or if available, use one ounce of washing soda per gallon of cool, clean water. Leave the pelts in the neutralizing solution for twenty minutes for a thin skin, and up to two hours for a thick, heavy skin.

RINSING THE PELTS

The pelts should then be rinsed at least two times in cool, clean water. Squeeze the water out of the skins after each rinsing. The pelts are then ready for stretching and drying.

DRYING, SOFTENING, AND STRETCHING THE TANNED PELTS

The methods for stretching the pelts are the same as described in the section on care of fur pelts or skins. Those cased are put on skin stretchers; those skinned open are laced in a frame or nailed out on a board.

LUBRICATING THE SKIN

After the skin has been dried for two to six hours, depending upon the thickness of the skin, apply a thin coat of neatsfoot oil, melted salt-free butter, or boot preservative oil, available at most department stores and shoe stores, to the flesh side of the skin. Use care along the edge of the skin and around the eye holes so the oil does not go into the hair. At 70°-75°F the oil will soak into the skin in six to twelve hours. After the first coat of oil has soaked into the skin, apply another thin coat of neatsfoot oil or leather dressing. Boot preservative oil works well and can be found in most shoe stores or department stores.

Let the oil soak in well. On heavy or thick hide, such as bear, apply another coat of oil around the neck and shoulders. The pelts are then ready to start the softening process.

DRYING AND SOFTENING TANNED LUBRICATED PELTS

The oiled skins are now ready for the final drying and softening. Put the cased skins back on their stretchers. Lay out the open skinned pelts flat on the floor. The drying time depends upon the thickness of the skin and fur, air temperature, and air movement. Drying is a very critical time in the custom tanning process. When the pelts start to show light colored areas on the skin, they must be worked. This is called "breaking the skins" to make them soft.

The breaking or working can be done on a "staking board." A staking board is rounded and beveled to one-sixteenth of an inch edge at the top. Small skins can be worked soft by hand as well as on a staking board. Stretch or work the skins in both directions until the entire skin is soft. If you are tanning a lot of skins at one time, work each skin a little bit, and then go back and work each skin a little more until they are all completely softened. Skins that are laced in a frame to dry after being lubricated can be softened somewhat by working them with a scraper.

Use sandpaper to obtain a smooth, uniform finish on the flesh side of the pelt. The thicker the skin, the coarser the sandpaper you use. Make sure that there are no wrinkles in the skin or small objects of any kind under the skin, or the sandpaper will cut a hole in the skin. If the skins are to be sewn, the sandpaper can also be used to cut the skins down to a uniform thickness.

CLEANING OR GLAZING THE FUR

If the fur on pelts or garments needs cleaning or becomes dull, work fine hardwood sawdust into the fur. Then shake out the sawdust and beat out the sawdust with a wooden stick. This will both clean and glaze the fur.

17

CHECKLIST OF PROCEDURES

1. WASH
Cool, clean water.
2. FLESH
Scrape off flesh, fat, and muscular coat.
3. WASH
To each gallon water: 1/4 cup powdered laundry detergent.
4. RINSE
Cool, clean water. Rinse several times to remove all detergent.
5. TAN
In plastic garbage can or plastic bucket to each gallon of water:
1 lb. salt
1 oz. concentrated sulphuric acid
CAUTION: ADD ACID AND SALT TO WATER SLOWLY TO
AVOID DANGEROUS SPLASHING.
6. NEUTRALIZE
To each gallon of water:
1 oz. borax or
1 oz. washing soda
Soak 20 minutes to 2 hours depending on skin thickness.
7. RINSE
Cool, clean water.
8. STRETCH
Lace to frame or nail to board. Dry 2 to 6 hours.
9. LUBRICATE
Apply neatsfoot oil to flesh side in warm room. Wait 10 to 12
hours. Apply neatsfoot oil or leather dressing. Wait until oil has
soaked into hide. Dry.
10. DRY AND SOFTEN
Stretch or work in both directions until skin is soft. Sand flesh
side to make it smooth or to thin down leather.

Types of Fleshing Beams

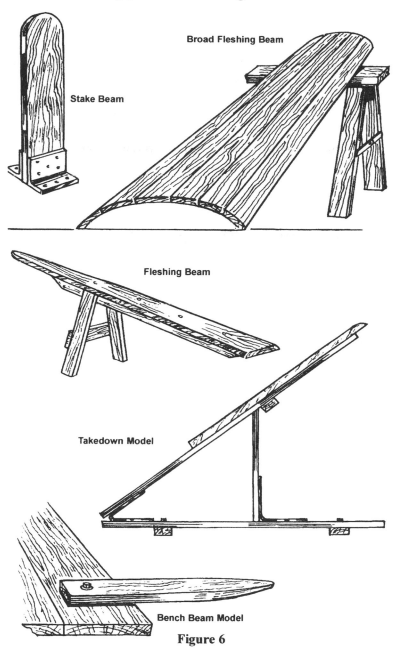

Stake Beam

Broad Fleshing Beam

Fleshing Beam

Takedown Model

Bench Beam Model

Figure 6

19

ALL ABOUT TRAPPING

TRAPPING

Trapping is one of the oldest of human occupations, and while it has for countless generations provided mankind with warm clothing, there's one objectionable element in it: the possibility of cruelty. Allowing animals to lie unattended in a steel trap is irresponsible. We should take care to see that no living thing suffers as a result of our neglect or heedless methods. Part of being a good woodsman is to follow the woodsman's code:

1. Visit often every trap you set—at the very least once a day, twice a day if possible.
2. Learn to set your traps in such a way that the animal will be killed almost instantly.

HOW TO KEEP A TRAP FROM FREEZING

Often enough in cold, snowy weather, ice will freeze around the trap trigger and prevent a catch when an otherwise good set has been made. But there is a way to prevent the trap from freezing.

Scoop out a depression in the snow, and place the trap in it. Underneath the trigger of the trap place a little piece of cotton cloth. This will absorb moisture from the trigger which consequently will not freeze and prevent the trap from springing. Over the entire trap and pan, place a sheet of oiled paper, folding it in around the edges of the trap. Then cover the area with leaves, sticks, or snow to look like its natural surroundings. You may be assured that the trap is safe against freezing in wet, cold weather.

Always bear in mind that materials used should be kept free from human scent, except in the case of skunk or muskrat. Skunks and muskrats are not trap shy, nor are they wary of human scent.

TRAPPING HINTS

While the ground is soft and there is still summer foliage on the trees, the trapper should cruise out his territory and find where furbearers are traveling. Muskrats, always a popular fur and fairly easy to catch, haunt the swamps and marshy places. They are nearly always to be found along the still waters of ponds and rivers . However, their pelts are late in priming and they should be trapped before early fall.

Skunks prime fairly early and usually bring fair prices. The mink is more wary than the muskrat and the skunk and is usually found in the fall traveling up and down small creeks or rivers. Before trapping mink you should boil your traps carefully in water mixed with lye or with hemlock tips. Mink are shy of steel scent and of human scent. So you must also wear gloves which have not touched anything that has even a slight flavor of human scent. The gloves should be boiled too, the same as the traps. Mink are always interested in any small hole. They will always investigate a hollow log lying on the bank of a river, and they are particularly interested in fish, especially trout.

The best mink scent is trout oil. This is made by cutting a couple of trout into small pieces and placing them in a glass jar. Stand the jar in the sun, leaving it there until the trout have decayed and the oil begins to form. You now have a scent that is very appealing to mink.

EQUIPMENT

Suggested equipment for trapping includes the following:
1. Traps—suitable sizes according to kinds of animals
2. Hatchet or hand axe—necessary for cutting stakes and also useful as a digging tool

3. Hand trowel or small shovel-convenient for making hole sets and removing dirt
4. Piece of old canvas or other similar material 3 by 4 feet for kneeling on while making dirt sets and for removing excess dirt
5. Sifting box made from ⅛-inch hardware cloth for replacing dirt on traps set for fox, coyote, and badger
6. Wire, size # 9 and # 14, for securing traps and making drowning rigs
7. Wire cutter pliers
8. Trap pan covers—cut from scraps of cloth. A discarded pair of old overalls, or similar material, is good for this purpose.
9. Quart jar with lid for carrying baits, lures, and scents.
10. Pair of light canvas or cotton gloves
11. A light pack basket or pack board—handy for carrying your equipment

Following are specific sets for the more common furbearers. There are many variations of these sets and though only a few are described here, the novice will gain a great deal by using these basic sets as guides and devising his own variations as he becomes more proficient with experience.

TREATING TRAPS

Many trappers like to treat their traps to remove newness, oil film, and human scent. The following method is satisfactory for this purpose.

Place traps in a tub or bucket of water that contains one can of lye to every ten gallons of water. The use of lye is not necessary but will aid in grease and oil removal. **Caution: Lye is very caustic. Be sure you use it with care, and not around children.**

Place the trap rings between the jaws to hold them open during the cleaning and coloring process. Boil the traps until all factory grease is gone; then dump them on the ground and let them lie a few days until they become heavy with rust. Remove the rust with a wire brush, and boil the traps in clean water for a few minutes. Make a batch of bark tea by boiling about a gallon of bark chips in two gallons of water. Boil the cleaned traps in this tea until they turn a bluish-black; then hang them up in a clean place until they are to be used.

Waxing the traps helps prevent rusting and also helps keep traps operating freely in freezing weather. If you want to wax your traps, place three cakes of petroleum wax in two to three gallons of boiling water. Dip the traps into the water, and allow time for them to become hot. Remove the traps by lifting them slowly from the bucket, leaving a thin coating of wax on their surface.

TYPES OF SETS

THE CUBBY SET

Animals such as mink, skunks, weasels, bobcats, and foxes can be taken with a cubby set. A cubby may be made of rocks or logs, or it may be a natural formation that could be used with or without modification. These sets have the advantage of protecting traps during bad weather. Cubbies may be blind (closed) or tunnel-like (open).

BLIND SETS

It is often desirable to hide traps so that passing animals will step into them. The traps are buried in the ground or hidden in mud along a stream. Trip sticks are often helpful with blind sets, because an animal will not step on anything it can step over. Place a small stick, about two inches high, on either side of the concealed trap. The animal approaching one of the sticks, will step over it into the pan. Coyotes, beavers, foxes, minks, and raccoons may be trapped in this manner.

BAITED OR SCENTED SETS

These sets are usually just blind sets with some lure or scent to attract an animal. There are several good scent and lure preparations sold commercially. Two types of scents are used. One is a urine and/or scent gland preparation which attracts the attention of animals. The other type is a food scent, which will cause animals to search for bait. You may make your own; however, the beginning trapper will do well to use commercially prepared scents.

HOW TO SET A SCENT SET

1. Dig a trench 12 inches wide, 30 inches long, and 3 inches deep, and place excess dirt on the kneeling cloth.
2. When you set the traps, make sure the trap pan is level with the jaws. Bend the trap springs toward the trigger side so jaws will lie flat.
3. Bed the traps firmly at either end of the trench and hide the chain and drag in the middle of the trench.
4. Place the pan cover under the jaws, making certain the trigger release is free.
5. Cover the traps and firm the dirt with your fingers. Fill in the trench with loose dirt, leaving about 1/4 inch of dirt over the trap pan.
6. The fingers point out positions of the trap pans.
7. Place a few drops of scent on a dry piece of wood or old cow chip which is placed between the two traps. Smooth the set to blend with the surrounding ground. Re-scent your set every other day.

MINK

Blind sets are very successful for trapping mink. These sets may be located along a creek or stream where mink habitually enter and leave the water. A #2 coil spring trap hidden in shallow water and staked to drown any captured animal is very effective. If the stream is frozen, the trap may be hidden under loose debris or snow along a mink trail. Because mink cannot be drowned in this type of set, double-jawed traps such as the Victor #22 coil spring (or other brand; see reference list at the end of the book) are very good and will help prevent wring-outs.

Areas where feeder streams or springs flow into major streams are good locations for mink sets. If a suitable area is too wide, it may be narrowed down with willow brush or other sticks. Another good set for mink can be made by digging a hole into a stream bank. The hole should be about eight inches in diameter and three feet into a bank along a stream. The hole should be situated so that there are one or two inches of water in the bottom. A #22 coil spring is concealed inside the mouth of the hole and staked to drown a captured animal. Bait may be placed at the back of the hole and/or a few drops of scent placed eight to ten inches above the set on the end of a dry stick. If possible, stand in the water while making this type of set and splash water over the hole entrance after the set is completed. This will eliminate much of the human odor and give the hole a fresh appearance.

A hole set may be made as a dry land set with the trap covered by loose dirt or leaves and then scented. Many mink trappers wear rubber gloves to make mink sets. This is desirable, but not necessary if reasonable care is used to prevent excessive human odor from contaminating the set.

The cubby set also makes a good mink set. Construct a cubby so it is five to six inches wide, four to six inches high, and about eighteen inches long. Place a trap in the mouth of the cubby if a closed-type is used, and bait or scent the closed end. If a tunnel-type is used, place the trap in the center of the cubby, and bait or scent above the trap.

MUSKRATS

Tail drags in snow or mud

Muskrats are easily trapped. Traps may be placed in runs leading to houses or bank dens. It is unnecessary to conceal the trap. Excellent locations are next to feeding stations where traps may be staked in the water. Feeding stations are little mounds of mud, partially submerged rocks and logs, and bunches of grass and cattails along the water. Muskrats sit upon the stations while they feed or rest.

Another good set is made by placing a trap in the notch of a floating log, which muskrats use for landings. Nail the trap chain to the underside of the log. Embed the trap in mud, and the set is ready. On logs five to six feet long, two or three traps may be set in this manner. Apple, carrot, parsnip, or other raw vegetables or fruit may be used as bait, or a few drops of commercial muskrat lure may be placed at the back of or above the trap site.

When streams and marshes are frozen, chop holes through the ice and place traps in runs or den outlets. Traps may also be placed inside muskrat houses. Replace any part of the house cut away for placing the trap.

RACCOONS

Raccoons are strong animals, and a size two or three trap should be used. Dry-land sets are made by burying a trap next to a trail used by raccoons. Use fine, dry soil or leaves to conceal the trap. Traps are concealed much the same as coyote or fox sets. Some fish oil or oil of anise is a good lure to use on these sets. Old stumps and logs next to a stream are ideal places to look for raccoon signs, and a set may be made near them.

A dirt-hole set made exactly like that for fox and coyotes can be used effectively on raccoons. Bait with fish oil, oil of anise, or a commercially prepared raccoon scent. Wire and stake the traps securely.

Water sets are made by placing a trap in three or four inches of water. Cover the trap with mud, and bait with oil of anise, fish oil or a commercial lure. Find a place where tracks indicate raccoons are entering or leaving the water. Use guide or trip sticks to guide animals into traps. A dry spot within a stream bank is a good place to set for raccoon. The set may be made either by placing the trap on a rock and baiting, or it may be made along the stream bank. All water sets should be rigged to drown a captured animal. Water sets made for raccoons often take mink and muskrats, so are valuable dual-purpose sets.

SKUNKS

Skunks are easy to trap. A small cubby set made with rocks and baited with canned sardines is very effective. A size 1 1/2 trap with double jaws is recommended for skunks. Traps placed near the openings of small culverts will take skunks. Sardines nailed to a fence post with a trap beneath it is satisfactory. The trap need not be covered.

If a large quantity of bait is available, such as a dead calf, bucket of chicken heads, or like material, cover the bait with leaves or light trash. Place three or four traps around this bait and toggle them with drags. A rock placed on the outside of a trap away from the bait is an excellent guide to insure that the skunk steps on the pan. Several animals may be taken during a single night in this manner.

BOBCATS

Cubby sets are good for taking bobcats. Bobcat cubbies should be quite large and can be made of rocks and or logs. The opening should be from one to two feet wide and at least two feet high. A #4 trap buried in the snow or hidden under loose debris or leaves and wired securely is preferred. Some trappers like to use two traps.

Bobcats depend more on their keen eyesight than on their sense of smell to locate their food. A dead rabbit, tied securely in the cubby behind the traps, makes a good bait. Some commercial cat scent or oil of catnip may be used along with the bait. Place a few drops in the back of the cubby. Bobcats travel considerable distances in search for food, so don't expect a catch every night.

BEAVERS

Traps set for beavers may be placed at the bottom of beaver slides or runs. These are paths along streams that beavers make to get from the water to their food supply on land. Place the trap in about four to eight inches of water just below and slightly to one side of the point where a slide enters the water. The traps should be heavily weighted or wired to a drowning device. Bait on green willow, cottonwood, or aspen twigs is stuck in the mud above the trap. Scent may also be used and should be placed on a dry stick about twelve to eighteen inches above the hidden trap.

Another beaver set may be made by placing traps in runs under water, or traps may be placed in dens or house openings. Guide sticks may be necessary. No bait or scent is used for this type of set.

Trapping under ice in winter is more difficult but can be done by wiring the trap to a stout, dry pole. Do not use a green pole, because beavers may chew it. The traps are placed on a platform fastened to the pole. Bait sticks may be nailed or wired to the pole about twelve inches above the trap. This set is particularly good around a cache (food pile). Traps may be wired to a platform which is fastened to the pole, or placed on the bottom of the stream or pond. Fasten bait to the pole as explained above.

When using a dry pole set, stick the end of the pole firmly in the mud, leaving the other end sticking above the ice. The pole will freeze solid, and no drowning rig is needed. A beaver is a very strong animal, and traps should be anchored securely.

THE #330 CONIBEAR TRAP FOR BEAVER

The #330 Conibear trap is quite effective for taking beaver through the ice. Two methods seem to give satisfactory results.

1. Set and bait the trap, and suspend it through a hole cut in the ice beside a cache. A stick to suspend the trap is wired to the trap chain and placed across the hole. Best results seem to be obtained when the trap is barely touching the bottom of the stream or pond.

2. Set and bait the trap as explained above. Wire the trap to a stout, dry pole. Position the trap on the pole so that when the lower end of the pole is pushed into the mud the trap will just be touching the bottom. The top of the pole should protrude through the hole in the ice and will freeze in place overnight. The #330 Conibear trap can be set in runs or den openings where there is no ice.

Fox   **Coyote**

COYOTE AND FOX

The most common sets for these animals are the scent-post set and the dirt-hole set. These are illustrated later in this book. A size 3-N trap is recommended for coyotes and foxes. If only foxes are trapped, the #2 coil spring trap is excellent.

If there is snow on the ground, traps may be buried in the snow and a scent post provided just as with sets where traps are placed in soil. Use care to brush away your tracks after making a snow set.

When the ground is frozen, a dirt-hole set can be made with dry dirt from an ant hill or litter from a chicken house. Any dry dirt is satisfactory. A trench twelve by thirty inches for foxes and twelve by thirty-six inches for coyotes is chipped out of the frozen ground about three inches deep and an inch-and-a-half to two inches of dry dirt placed in it. Set traps on this in exactly the same way as in the regular scent post set just described. Re-scent the area every two or three days.

Another method for setting traps in snow is to kick away the snow in an area ten to fifteen feet in diameter. Pour dry dirt on the ground and set as a normal scent post or dirt-hole set. Don't be concerned about disturbing the animals by kicking the snow, because it actually seems to attract the attention of animals.

MARTEN

These mink-sized animals inhabit the wild mountain areas. Marten are agile tree-climbers; consequently a common practice is to set a # 1 or # 2 1/2 trap in a notch cut in a large tree. Marten trapping is usually done during deep snow conditions, and the sets should be made well above the high snow line. Pine squirrel's or smoked fish make good bait for marten sets. Traps need not be covered but should be fastened so that an animal, after being caught, will hang away from the tree.

PLACING TRAPS

Trapping conditions will vary from set to set, but the basic fundamentals for placing traps will remain the same. All traps must be placed on a firm footing so they will not move or give if an animal steps on a part other than the pan. When making a dirt set, stabilize the traps by placing soil around the springs and jaws, packing it with your fingers. This is particularly important when making coyote and fox sets, for if an animal steps on a trap and it gives, he may suspect a mouse and dig up the trap.

When placing traps under water or in wet or oozy mud, make sure that there is no mud or other obstruction under the pan. A rock, old board, or other solid object will make a firm platform for a trap bed. Place the footing about two inches below the desired trap level. This affords a firm base but provides room for hiding the trap.

Traps should be placed so animals enter from the hinge ends of the traps. Traps set in holes or cubbies should be placed with the springs toward the back side and away from the approach as much as possible. Always bend the springs on long-spring type traps toward the dog, or trigger, sides at about a 45-degree angle so the free jaw may lie flat. Adjust the pans so they lie flat and level with the jaws when the traps are set. Fasten traps securely or use drag hooks, whichever is appropriate.

DROWNING RIGS

Often, it will be advisable to set traps so captured animals will be drowned. Beaver, mink, raccoon, and muskrat sets are usually placed in this manner. A one-way slip can be made, or large weights tied closely to the traps. This will weight the animals down in deep water. The weights should be about as heavy as the animals you intend to trap. Drowning stakes are also effective in keeping animals in deep water so they will drown. A downward loop can be fashioned from #9 wire and anchored in deep water. The trap ring is placed over the wire so it will slip down and become caught in the loop. When an animal is caught in a trap, it usually jumps for water. This should be its last jump. When trapping under ice, no drowning device is needed.

SOME TRAPPING IDEAS

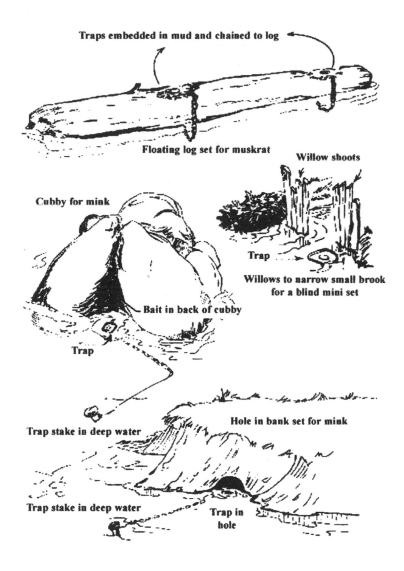

Traps embedded in mud and chained to log

Floating log set for muskrat

Willow shoots

Cubby for mink

Trap

Willows to narrow small brook
for a blind mini set

Bait in back of cubby

Trap

Trap stake in deep water

Hole in bank set for mink

Trap stake in deep water

Trap in
hole

Figure 7

GENERAL PELT CARE

Many thousands of dollars are lost each year by trappers who do not properly care for pelts. As mentioned earlier, factors affecting the value of a pelt are its primeness and the way it is stretched, skinned, and tailored in preparation for sale.

There are several important steps from trap to pocketbook. A pelt, in order to command the highest price, must be properly skinned, fleshed, stretched, and dried.

The proper care of any pelt begins immediately after an animal is caught. Often, trappers will stockpile animals in a garage or barn for several days before skinning them. This is not advisable. The sooner pelts are removed from carcasses, the better their quality will be and the better they will stretch. Animals not skinned for several days may become dirty, the fur may start to slip, and grease burns may develop. Animals stored in a barn or cellar may also be exposed to vermin damage.

At times, trappers find they must skin furbearers where they are caught in order to reduce carrying weight. In this case, the pelts should be rolled up, skin-side in, until they can be stretched and dried. Pelts which are stretched open should be folded in half with the skin side in and then rolled for carrying.

It is best not to allow carcasses to freeze, but if this occurs, no attempt should be made to remove the pelts from frozen carcasses. Thaw them slowly in a cool place (40°-60°F) before skinning. All dirt, mud, and blood should be washed from the fur before animals are skinned.

The state of primeness is indicated by the skin side of pelts. If the skins contain dark areas or spots, or appear bluish in color, they are not prime and consequently are decreased in value. Prime pelts look clean and whitish in color with absolutely no dark areas or patches. These pelts command premium prices.

SKINNING

The prime requisite for skinning any animal is a sharp knife. Many trappers, especially beaver trappers, prefer three knives:

1. A thin bladed one for cutting the skin from chin to tail.
2. A heavy one for removing the feet.
3. One for removing the pelt.

The pelting knife must be kept razor sharp, as it is almost impossible to skin any animal, especially beaver, with anything else. Obviously any cuts in a pelt will greatly reduce its market value, and a dull knife tends to cause pelt cuts.

A table or platform of convenient height is a great help. A 50-gallon drum topped with a wooden platform makes a very good skinning table. A wooden trough made from two 4-foot lengths of 1- by 8-inch lumber mounted on sawhorse-type legs of convenient height is excellent for use in skinning beaver as well as other animals. Care should be taken to prevent blood or fat from getting on the fur. Paper towels or rags are very handy for wiping up excess blood and dirt and for keeping the skin side clean.

FLESHING

Fleshing is the removal of all excess fat, grease, and muscle tissue from skins. This prevents fat burns and facilitates proper drying and stretching. Fat burns are caused by the chemical breakdown of fatty tissue, which causes the hair roots to loosen and fall out when the pelt is processed. Obviously, this will reduce the quality of the fur and consequently the ultimate market value of the pelt.

Proper fleshing of pelts is very important in maintaining their value. For best results, it should be done at the time of skinning. Fleshing afterwards often results in damaged skins and is more time consuming. All fat, and in most cases all muscle tissue, must be removed from the pelts.

Different animals require slightly different techniques and will be discussed individually later.

There are many fleshing tools available commercially, and any good trapper's supply catalog lists such items as draw knife, vise flesher, and gambrel hooks. These items are not necessary but may save considerable time for the busy trapper.

There are many fleshing tools available commercially, and any good trapper's supply catalog lists such items as draw knife, vise flesher, and gambrel hooks. These items are not necessary but may save considerable time for the busy trapper.

CLEANING PELTS

Another process often overlooked by trappers is cleaning or washing furs and pelts before they are stretched to be dried. A solution mild soap and water is satisfactory for this purpose. Rinse thoroughly and remove the excess water. This will wash away dirt, mud, and other foreign matter and give the pelts a fine appearance. If there is blood on the fur, rinse it off in cold water before using the soap solution. Soap tends to set the blood, making removal difficult. Pelts, especially those of beaver, should be washed in a solution of borax.

STRETCHING PELTS

Stretching or "tailoring" methods will vary for each kind of animal. prefer to use their own homemade stretching boards. Experience alone will tell the skinner how large the stretching boards should be, but measurements for various kinds are listed for use as a guide. After stretching, pelts should be dried with a paper towel or cloth and wiped clean. Any remaining fat must be removed at this time.

DRYING AND STORING PELTS

After pelts are put on a stretching board or wire, they should be placed in a dry room, ideally with a temperature between 70° and 75°F The most important requirements are that the room be above freezing and free from any dampness. An attic over a warm room is an ideal place for drying pelts. Never store or dry pelts in a damp basement or cellar, and keep them away from direct sunlight and artificial heat of any kind.

As the pelts dry, brush the fur to improve their appearance and help remove any remaining fat particles. (In the case of beaver or raccoon pelts nailed to solid boards, brushing cannot be performed until the pelts are removed.) Also, some additional dressing or fleshing will improve the quality of most pelts during the stretching and drying process. Here again, caution must be used to prevent any knife damage to the skins.

After pelts are thoroughly dried, they may be removed from the stretching boards and stored until sold. Tie them together at the top and suspend them from a rafter or beam where they will be free from rodent and vermin damage. At this time, pelts that are stretched with the fur exposed should be combed out with a stiff brush to improve the appearance and further remove any foreign matter. A properly dried pelt needs no further attention. Never stack pelts on top of each other. When they are shipped, always place open pelts fur-to-fur and skin-to-skin. This will prevent oil and grease from getting on the fur.

INDIVIDUAL PELT HANDLING

Mink, weasel, and marten are pelted "cased" (removed without opening the hide down the belly). The pelt is removed by first making cuts as shown by pictures in this book "peeling" or pulling the pelt from the carcass. The hind feet are split down the bottoms and the bones and flesh of the feet removed. Toenails and pads of the feet are left on the pelt.

The tail should be split. This cut is begun on the underside of the tail root (where it joins the body) and carried entirely to the tip. An umbrella stave may be inserted in the tail and the crease in the stave stave used as a guide for the cut. A razor blade is also good for splitting the tail but is slower, and care must be used not to cut the fur or make a crooked cut.

If the tail is not split, the bone must be removed. Two small boards, each about 1 by 4 by 1/4 inches thick, are used for this purpose. Skin down the tail for an inch or so with a knife or razor blade. Place the two boards one on each side of the tail. Holding the boards firmly against the tailbone, pull away from the body toward the end of the tail. The edges of the boards will force the pelt from the tail. Pull the pelt over the carcass and, if necessary, use a sharp knife to remove any fat or excess muscle from it.

There will be a band of muscle tissue stuck tightly to the pelt around the middle of the back, belly, and shoulders. This may be left on, provided no fat is permitted to remain with it. Removal of this thin band of muscle from the pelt is very difficult without cutting the skin. For this reason, most fur buyers prefer to have this band left on the skin of the marketed pelt.

Next, pull the pelt from the front feet, being careful to skin out the toes, leaving only the toe-pads and toenails. Be careful around the ears, eyes, and nose, making certain that the eyelids, lips, and ears remain on the pelt. Remove any remaining fat, and thoroughly clean the pelt of mud and blood. Now turn the pelt right-side-out and make certain no blood or dirt is on the fur. Pull the pelt, fur-side-in, over the proper sized board. These boards may be made from one-quarter-inch stock, sanded smooth, and about one-third longer than the pelt and tail in order to permit easy handling. The width of the stretching boards will vary depending upon the kind and size of the pelt, but an average-sized male mink stretching board will be about 4 1/2 inches wide at the bottom and about 38 inches long.

Only experience can indicate just how tightly to stretch the pelt, but pull it fairly snugly and tack the open end to the board. The tail can be tacked out flat if split, or one small nail can be used in the end of the tail to hold it straight from the pelt while drying. Some trappers tack a small mesh hail screen over the tail to hold it flat and straight while drying. Treat the skins as directed under "DRYING AND STORING PELTS."

Marten pelts are treated the same as are mink and weasel, with the exception that marten pelts are turned fur-side-out after they have dried a bit. This must be done before the pelt is too dry, or it will crack and lose value.

MUSKRATS

Muskrats are skinned and stretched much the same as mink except that the feet and tail are cut off at the fur line. Remove excess fat and muscle tissue from the pelts. Here again the thin band of muscle should be left on the pelts just as in the case of mink, weasel, and marten. Muskrat pelts may be stretched on a board made for this purpose or on commercial wire stretchers. Dry and store as instructed under "DRYING AND STORING PELTS." Muskrats are easily skinned, but, as mentioned earlier, their skin is thin and easily torn.

OTTERS, FOXES, AND COYOTES

Coyotes and foxes are skinned and stretched cased, much like a mink or muskrat. The tail should be split down the under side or left uncut with the tailbone removed. Two boards, as described earlier, may be used for this purpose.

41

Otter, fox, and coyote skins are turned fur-side-out after they have dried for a day or two. As with other furs, removal of all fat and excess muscle tissue is essential to insure top quality pelts. Brushing the fur during and immediately after drying will improve its appearance and help the drying process. After the pelts have been removed from stretching boards and turned fur-side-out, hang them up on a wire or string passed through the nose, and place a small board inside the pelts to hold them open for continued drying. Store the pelts as previously described.

BOBCATS

Bobcat pelts are removed cased. The toes and claws should be left on the pelts. As bobcat skins are fairly tough, much of the skinning may be done by merely pulling the pelts from the carcasses. A knife is used to skin around the head, and care must be taken to ensure that the ears and nose remain on the pelts.

Fleshing may be done with the aid of a fleshing board after the pelts are removed from the carcasses. However, if no fleshing board is available, fold a burlap bag in fourths, place it over your knee, and place the pelt on top. All fat and excess muscle tissue may then be cut away with a sharp knife.

Place the fleshed pelts fur-side-in over stretching boards and allow them to dry from one to two days. At this time the pelts are removed, turned fur-side-out, then replaced on the stretching boards and hung up to complete drying as directed for fox and coyote pelts. Store as directed under "DRYING AND STORING PELTS."

BADGERS AND RACCOONS

Badgers are skinned "open" like beavers, but the pelts are stretched square instead of round. Raccoons are stretched cased with the leather side out. These animals tend to be quite fat and will require considerable attention while fleshing and skinning. All fat and muscle tissue should be removed and the skin-side wiped clean with a cloth and washed if necessary. This may be done after the pelts are nailed to stretching boards and will help remove any remaining fat and oil from the hides.

When nailing one of these pelts to a board (which may be any convenient size as long as it is sturdy), begin by tacking all four feet out on a rough square. Pull the belly skin out sideways in line with the feet and tack in place. Continue nailing by halving each nail distance around the edge of the hide. The nose of the pelt may rise slightly above the straight line between the front feet, but this is acceptable if not too extreme.

It may be necessary to relocate the nails originally placed in the feet in order to maintain desired squareness of pelts. Nails in the finished pelts will be one-half to one-fourth inches apart and about one-fourth from the edge of the pelts. Any small irregular edges may be trimmed, but if skinning and stretching is done properly, this will seldom be necessary.

BEAVERS

Beavers are the most difficult of furbearers to skin and stretch properly. This is primarily because the pelts cannot be pulled from carcasses like muskrat or mink, but must be removed almost entirely by cutting away with a sharp knife.

Before skinning begins, all mud, dirt, blood, and other foreign matter should be washed from the fur. The beaver is placed on its back and cuts made around the feet and tail at the hair line. Some trappers use an axe to remove the feet and while this method may save some time, it also may result in damaged pelts. Therefore, a stout, sharp knife is preferred. The tail may or may not be left on the carcass during skinning. Next, make a cut from the tip of the lower jaw down the mid-belly line, branching along the hair line around the anus and continuing so as to join the cut made around the tail. Grasp the pelt at the belly with one hand, and start cutting it free from the carcass. Continue this on one side of the pelt around to the middle of the back, turning the beaver slightly if needed. Then, again starting at the belly, remove the remaining half of the pelt in the same manner.

Beaver pelts require more care and time than most pelts, but a properly tailored beaver will reward the trapper for his extra effort. Prices are determined by primeness, quality, and size of the pelt. Measurements are determined by adding the nose-to-tail length to the width.

STEPS FOR SKINNING BEAVERS
1. A cut is made from the tip of the lower jaw to the tail. Feet and tail are removed.
2. The pelt is cut from the carcass, beginning at the belly.
3. The carcass is turned as the pelt is removed.
4. Detail showing removal of pelt from leg, leaving a hole in the pelt.
5. Use care in cutting around ears, eyes, and mouth.
6. Additional fleshing may be necessary after pelt is removed. A burlap bag may be folded and placed over the knee for this job.

BEAVER CASTORS
Beaver castors are another source of income from animals. Properly dried castors are marketed and used to produce scents, lures, and even costly perfumes. Castors are located in the body cavity, just forward and to either side of the anal opening. They appear as wrinkled elongated sacs, connected together, and joined by the adjacent oil sacs. The castors and oil sacs are removed as one piece, the oil sacs

are carefully removed from the wrinkled castors, the castors are twisted shut to prevent loss of the castoreum, then either hung over a wire or laid out on any horizontal surface to dry. The oil sacs have little or no commercial value but can be retained for making bait scents. Take care not to puncture the castors, because their contents give them their value. Beaver castors should be completely dry before selling.

ALL ABOUT DEADFALLS AND SNARES

DEADFALLS AND SNARES

BUILDING DEADFALLS

During the centuries that trapping has been carried on, not only in America, but throughout the entire world, various kinds of traps and snares have been in use. In all regions homemade traps, that is, deadfalls and snares rather than steel traps, are used a great deal.

"The number of furs caught each year is largely by homemade traps," said a trapper some years ago who has spent upwards of forty years in the forests and is well acquainted with traps, trappers, and fur-bearing animals. One thing is certain, however, and that is that many of the men who have spent years in trapping and have been successful use deadfalls and snares as well as steel traps.

Another trapper said, "In my opinion trapping is an art, and any trapper that is not able to make and set a through out, when occasion demands, does not belong to the profession." (A through out is a trap which leads an animal to attempt to walk into it and pass through the back. However, it is constructed in such a way that the animal is actually unable to escape once inside.)

Here are a few of the many reasons why deadfalls are a good choice.

1. There is no weight to carry.
2. Many of the best trappers use them.
3. It requires no capital to set a line of deadfalls.
4. There is no loss of traps by trap thieves, but the fur is in as much danger.
5. Deadfalls do not mangle animals or injure their fur.
6. It is a humane way of killing animals.
7. There is no loss by animals twisting off a foot or leg and getting away.
8. Animals are killed outright, having no chance to warn others of their kind by their cries from being caught.

9. Trappers always have the necessary outfit (axe and knife) with them to make and set a through out that will kill the largest animals.
10. The largest deadfalls can be made to spring easily and catch small game if required.
11. Through outs will kill skunk without leaving any scent.
12. Deadfalls cost little or nothing.

It is a safe proposition, however, that not one-half of the trappers of today can build a through out properly or know how to make snares, and many of them have not so much as seen one.

Following is a storehouse of information on various deadfalls and snares, gleaned from trappers far and wide, even spanning generations. In many cases, the instructions given remain worded in their own styles.

One type of deadfall is made like this: First, a little pen about a foot square is built of stones, chunks, or by driving stakes close to together, leaving one side open. The stakes should be cut about thirty inches long and driven into the ground about fourteen inches, leaving about sixteen inches above the ground. Of course, if the earth is very solid, stakes need not be so long but should be so driven that only about sixteen inches remains above ground. A sapling about four inches in diameter and four feet long is laid across the end that is open. Another sapling four, five, or six inches in diameter, depending on what you are trying to trap, and about twelve feet long, is now cut for the "fall."

Stakes are set so that this pole, or fall, will play over the short pole on the ground. These stakes should be driven in pairs; two about eighteen inches from the end; two about fourteen inches farther back. (See Figure 8.)

The small end of the pole should be split and a small but stout stake driven firmly through it so there will be no danger of the pole turning and "going off" of its own accord. The trap is set by placing the prop (which is only seven inches in length and half an inch in diameter) between the top log and the short one on the ground, to which is attached the long trigger, which is only a stick about the size of the prop, but about twice as long, the baited end of which extends back into the little pen.

The bait may consist of a piece of chicken, rabbit, or any tough bit of meat as long as it is fresh, and the bloodier the better. When an animal smells the bait, it will reach into the trap top of the pen which was carefully covered over between the logs. When the animal seizes the bait, the long trigger is pulled off the upright prop, and down comes the fall, killing the animal by its weight. Skunk, coon, opossum, mink, and nearly all other kinds of animals are easily caught in this trap. Foxes are an exception, as it is rather hard to catch them in deadfalls. They tend to be more cautious and aware of their surroundings.

The more care that you take to build the pen tight and strong, the less likely is some animal to tear it down and get bait from the outside; also if you will cover the pen with leaves, grass, and sticks, animals will not be as wary of the trap. The triggers are very simple, the long one being placed on top of the upright, or short. The long triggers have a short prong left or a nail driven in it to prevent the game from getting the bait off too easily. If the saplings available are too small and light for a deadfall, they can be weighted with a pole.

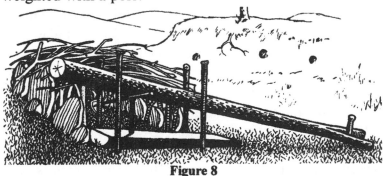

Figure 8

Here is one type of "through out" deadfall that has been used for many years, with much success. As you will see in Figure 9, the through out is constructed of stakes and rocks as follows: Select a place where there is game; you need an axe, some nails, also strong string, and a pole four inches or more in diameter. As labeled, No. 1 is the drop pole, which should be about six to seven feet long. No. 2 is the trip stick, No. 3 is string tied to pole and trip stick, No. 4 is the stakes for holding up the weight, No. 5 is the small stakes driven around in the shape of the letter *U*, which should be one foot wide and two feet long. No. 6 is the rocks, No. 7 is the bait.

Figure 9

This is a great trap for taking skunk, mink, and coon. It can be built quickly where there are small saplings and rocks.

The trapper's success depends entirely upon his skill, and no one can expect the best returns unless his work is skillfully done. Do not attempt to make that through out unless you are certain that you can make it right, and do not leave it till you are certain that it could not be any better made. One trapper wrote that he had seen deadfalls so poorly made and improperly set that they would make angels weep, neither were they located where game was apt to travel. The through out, if made right and located where game frequents, is quite successful.

As one old-time trapper admonished, "Boys, think out every little plan before you attempt it. If someone you know sets his traps one way, see if you can improve on his plan and make it a little better. Do not rush blindly into any new scheme, but look at it on all sides and make yourself well acquainted with the merits and drawbacks of it. Make good use of your brains, for the animal instinct is its only protection, and it is only by making good use of your reasoning powers that you can fool the animal. Experience may cost money sometimes and loss of patience and temper, but in my estimation it is the trapper's best capital. An old trapper who has a couple of traps and lots of experience will catch more fur than the greenhorn with a complete outfit. Knowledge is power, in trapping as in all other trades."

The "pinch-head" deadfall (see Figure 10) is the most merciful type, because the animal is killed instantly without suffering. Get some short pieces of board or short poles and lay them on the stones in the back part of the pen and on the raised stick in front. Lay them close together so the animal cannot crawl in at the top. Then get some heavy stones and lay them on the cover to weight down and throw

Figure 10

Note the "figure 4" trigger (shape of a number 4) set on this Pinch Head trap designed to be used without bait. For greater detail of the "figure 4" trigger, see Figure 10a.

some dead weeds and grass over the pen and triggers, and your trap is complete. When the animal tries to enter and sets off the trap by pressing against the long trigger in front, he brings the weighted pole down in the middle of his back, which soon stops his earthly career.

This through out can also be used at runways, that is, walking paths, with no bait. No pen or bait is required. The

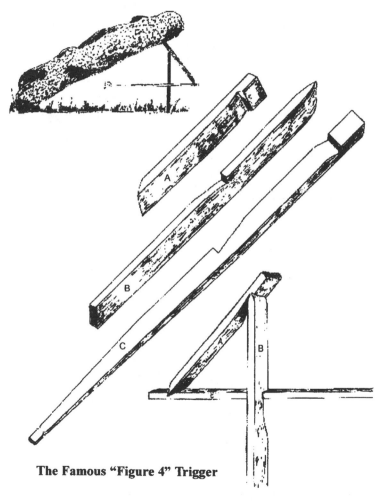

The Famous "Figure 4" Trigger

Figure 10a

game will be caught coming from either direction. The trap is "thrown" by the trigger or pushing against it when passing through. During snowstorms the trap requires considerable attention to keep in perfect working order but at most other times is quite reliable.

The trap can also be used at dens without bait with success. If used with bait it should be placed a few feet from the den or near any place frequented by the animal or animals you expect to catch.

Of course we all admit the steel trap is more convenient and up-to-date, acknowledged a New Hampshire trapper. You can make your sets faster and can change the steel trap from place to place; of course, the through out you cannot. But all this does not signify the through out is no good; it is good, especially for trapping mink. To the trapper who traps in the same locality every year, when his deadfalls are built once, it is only a few minutes' work to put them in shape; then he has got a trap for the season.

The Log Trap through out (also called Board or Pole Trap), when properly made and baited, is one of the best mink catchers in the trap line ever devised. This trap requires about an hour to make. The tools required are a camp hatchet and a good strong jack-knife, also a length of strong twine. All trappers should have as part of their standard equipment a ball of good, strong twine.

This trap should be about fifteen inches wide with a pen built with sticks or pieces of boards driven in the ground. (See Figure 11.) The jaws of this trap consist of two pieces of board three inches wide and about three and a half feet long, resting edgeways one on the other, held firmly by four posts driven in the ground. The top board, or drop, should move easily up and down before weights are put on. The treadle should be set three inches inside, level with the top of the bottom board. This is a round stick about three-fourths inches in diameter, resting against two pegs driven in the ground. The lever should be the same in size. Now put the sturdy string around the top board. Then set by passing the lever through the string over the cross piece and latching it in front of the treadle. Then put on weights and adjust to spring, heavy or light as desired. This trap should be set around old dams or log jams by the brook, baited with fish, muskrat, rabbit, or chicken.

Figure 11

Board or Pole Trap: Note the upright poles around the trap force the animal to enter from the front to get the bait and thus trip the trigger on the way into the trap.

Figures 12 and 13 show two types of through outs that can be used to catch bait meat. A snare can be used on the through out at the same time by putting the drop or weight where it isn't likely to fall on the animal. Put the weight on the other side of the tree or make it fall pushing the animal to one side. In this case a log must be used. A good sized rock is effective for small animals. The closer spikes 1 and 2 are together, and the longer the tugger end on bottom, the easier it will pull off.

Referring to Figure 12, the first spike (1) is driven into the tree one-half inch deeper than the other spike (2), to allow for the notch. (Nails make good spikes.) The other labels refer to the following:

3 - Bait on end of trigger.

4 - Heavy rock or log.

5 - Wire, fine soft steel.

6 -Trigger with notch cut in it.

7 - Notch cut in trigger (6). Spike 2 must have head cut off and pounded flat on end.

Figure 12
Bait Set

Figure 13
Bait Set

In setting the trap across a trail, as in Figure 13, drive a peg into the ground. The spikes are driven into this peg instead of the tree as in Figure 12. The parts are labeled as follows:

1 - Trail.

2 - Log.

3 - Trigger same as for bait in Figure 12.

4 - Stake driven in ground with spikes driven in it.

5 - Spikes same as Figure 12.

6 - Wire.

7 - Tree.

8 - Brush put in trail with one end between trigger and peg to knock off trigger when touched.

The end of the brush stick is set in between the peg and trigger end, and when an animal comes either way it will knock the brush and it knocks out the trigger. Good, soft steel wire should be used. In setting this through out along a river bank, drive a stout stick into the bank so it will hang out over the water. This stick will take the place of a tree limb. One end of a pole held in a slanting position by weighing one end down with a rock will do the same as a limb on a tree. If there is no convenient limb on the tree, lean a stout pole up against the tree and cut notches in it to hold the wire.

This through out has proven very successful. When trapping in parts of the country where lynx, coyote, or wolverine are likely to eat marten in traps, use a snare, and it will hang the game high and out of reach. Fasten the snare to the trigger.

BEAR AND COON

"I will explain how to make the best bear through out, also the best one for coon that ever was made," wrote an old and successful through out trapper. "First get a pole six to eight feet long for a bed piece, get another sixteen to eighteen feet long, and lay it on top of the bed piece. Now drive two stakes, one on each side of the bed piece and pole and near one end of the bed piece. About eighteen to twenty inches from the first two stakes, drive two more stakes, one on each side of the bed piece and fall pole. Now drive two more stakes directly in front of your two back stakes and about two inches in front.

"Next cut a stick long enough to come just to the outside of the last two stakes driven. Then whittle the ends off square so it will work easy between the treadle stakes and the two inside stakes that your fall works in; next raise your fall pole about three feet high. Get a stick about one inch through, and cut it so that it will be long enough to rest against your treadle. That short stick is your treadle when it

58

is raised above the bed piece. Cut the end off at a slant so it will fit well against the treadle.

"Slant the other end so the fall pole will fit well. Now five or six inches from the top of the slanted stick, cut a notch in your slanted stick. Go to the back side, lift your pole up, and set the post on the bed piece. Place the top of the slanted stick against the fall pole. Then place the pole off the post in the notch in the slant stick. Press back on the bottom of the slanted stick, and place your treadle against the stick. Your trap is set. Make a V shape on the inside of the treadle by driving stakes in the ground, and hedge it in tightly all around if possible. Cover the top tightly. The cubby should be three feet long, three feet high, and as wide as your treadle stakes.

"Stake the bait near the back end of the cubby. Be sure the treadle is just above the bed piece. Take the pole off the cubby to set the trap as you have set it from this side. You can set it heavy or light by regulating the treadle. I sometimes drive spikes in the bed piece and file them off sharp as it will hold better. You can weight the fall poles as much as you like after it is set. Don't you see, boys, that the old fellow comes along and to go in he surely will step on the treadle. "Bang!" It's lowered, and you've got him.

"This is the best coon through out I ever saw. The fall pole for coon should be about fourteen inches high when set. Set it under trees or along brooks where you can see coon signs. Bait with frogs, crabs, fish, a piece of muskrat, or duck for coon. Build it much the same as for bear, only much smaller. You will find this a successful trap."

A Montana trapper said, "I will describe a through out for bear which I use, and which works the best of any I have tried. (See Figure 14.) I have two small trees about thirty inches apart. I cut a pole ten feet long for a bed piece and place it in front of the trees, then cut a notch in each tree about twenty-seven inches above the bed piece, and nail a strong piece across from one tree to the other in the notches. Cut a long pole five or six inches in diameter for the through out, place the large end on top of bed log, letting the end stick by the tree far enough to place on poles for weights.

"Then cut two stakes, drive on the outside of both poles, and fasten the top of the stakes to the trees one foot above the cross piece. Then on the inside, thirty inches from the trees, drive two more solid stakes about two feet apart and nail a piece across them six inches lower than the cross piece between the trees.

"Then cut a lever about three feet long and flatten one end, and a bait stick about two feet long. Cut two notches six inches apart, one square on the top and the other on the bottom, and both close to the top end of the bait stick.

"Fasten the bait on the other end and then raise up the through out by placing the lever stick across the stick nailed between the two trees, letting the end run six inches under the through out. Take the bait stick and hook the lower notch on the piece nailed on the two stakes and place the end of the lever in the top notch.

"Cut weights and place on each side until you think you have enough to hold any bear. Then put on as many more and it will be about right. (In other words, it will probably take more weights than you might guess, so use more just in case.)

"Stand up old tree trunks around the sides and back and lots of green brush on the outside. Arrange it so the animal won't be able to see the bait.

"This doesn't require a very solid pen. I drive about three short stakes in front and leave them one foot high, so when he pulls back they will come against him, and the set is complete. You can weight it with a ton of poles, and still it will spring easily. The closer together the two notches, the easier it will spring.

"This trap can be built lighter and is good for coon. In fact, it will catch other furbearers, but is not especially recommended for small animals, such as ermine and mink."

Figure 14

The stone deadfall here described is used by trappers wherever flat stones can be found and is a good trap to catch skunk, opossum, mink, and other small game. The trap is made as follows:

The "figure 4" trigger is best for this trap and is made this way: the standard (1) is made by cutting a stick five or six inches long out of hard wood and whittling it to a flat point, but blunt at one end; (2) is about five inches long with a notch cut within about one and one-half inches of the end and the other end made square so that it will fit in (3), which is the bait stick. This is only a straight stick sixteen or eighteen inches long, while the other end of the stick should have a small prong on it, a tack driven in, or something to hold the bait in position. The best way will be to tie the bait on also.

Find a flat stone weighing from fifty to one hundred pounds, depending upon what game you expect to trap. Select the place for the trap, and place a small, flat stone underneath so your game will be killed quickly and also so that the upright trigger will not sink into the ground. Lift up the large or upper stone, kneeling on one knee before the stone, resting the weight of the stone on the other. This leaves both hands free to set the trap. This is done by placing the triggers in the position shown in the illustration and then letting the stone down very easily on the triggers. You should keep your knee under the stone all the time until you see that it comes down easily and does not "go off" its own weight. The bait should always be put on before the trap is set. This trap will go off easily, and you must be careful that the bait you put on is not too heavy and will cause the trap to fall of its own accord.

This trap can be made to catch rabbits, which will come in handy to bait other traps for larger game. In trapping for rabbits bait with bits of apples, cabbage, or other raw vegetables or fruit.

This trap does not take long to make, as no pen needs to be built. The top stone is large enough to strike the animal, no matter where it is positioned when trying to get the bait. A stone two or three inches thick and thirty inches across and the same length or a little longer is about the proper size for skunk, opossum, and other medium-sized animals, but of course larger or smaller stones can be used, whatever you find convenient.

This trap consists of a flat piece of stone supported by three pieces of wood, the whole trouble being in making these three pieces right, and this can be done by carefully comparing the description here given with illustrations, whenever they are referred to (see Figure 15). The parts are all made of wood about three-eighths of an inch thick. In the illustration, part 1 is thirteen inches long, with notches about one-sixteenth of an inch deep cut in its upper side, two of the notches near together and at one end, and another four and a half inches from the first two. The latter notch should be cut a little, sloping across the stick.

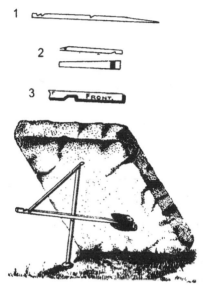

Figure 15

The part numbered 1 represents a top view, and the piece next below it is a side view as it should be made, and end farthest from the notches being trimmed to a point to hold the bait. This constitutes the trigger.

Part 2 is the lever, the upper drawing giving a side view and that below it a bottom view of this part of the trap. The piece of wood needed for it is six and one-half inches long, one inch wide at one end, and tapering down to three-sixteenths of an inch at the other; a notch is cut across the under side one and a half inches from the wide end.

Level off the upper side of the narrow end to about one-half the original thickness. If the flat stone to be used is a heavy one, the notch must not be more than one inch from the end; otherwise the leverage on the notches would be greater than is desirable, tending to hold the parts together too rigidly.

The upright post, part 3, is seven inches long, slightly forked at the bottom, to make it stand firm and prevent twisting around when in use, the upper end beveled from the front backwards at about a 45-degree angle. The front of the upright is the side that would face a person standing exactly opposite the trap when set.

On the right side cut a long notch, half the width of the wood in depth, starting at the hollow slope of the notch one inch in front of the lower end and making the square shoulder just three inches from the bottom of the post; level the shoulder off from the front so as to leave only a narrow edge. Place the post upright, the forked end standing on a small piece of wood or flat stone, to prevent it from sinking into the ground. Bait the pointed end of the trigger and hold it up horizontally with its middle notch catching behind the shoulder of the notch in the upright post; then place the beveled end of the lever in the notch at the end of the trigger, the notch in the lever lying on the edge of the top of the upright post.

Finally, rest the stone on the top of the lever, arranging the stone so that the bait will be near the lower end of the stone. (See Figure 16.)

It is a good plan to hollow out the ground somewhat under where the stone falls, to allow a space for the pieces of the "figure 4" to lie without danger of being broken. The bait, also, should be something that will flatten easily and not hard enough to tilt the stone up after it has fallen.

The trouble with most deadfalls usually set, is in the weight of the stone. When you find one heavy enough it

64

will not trip easily when game takes hold, and oftentimes
the sticks holding the deadfall collapse under the weight.
The head piece from the stone down to where the standard
sets in the notch should be fully 2 1/4 inches, so when the
stone starts to fall it throws triggers out from under; otherwise, the stone will catch and break them.

Figure 16

Note the "figure 4" shapes, and height of the stone.

Young trappers, when you are making triggers to prepare for your sets, tie each pair together separately as they are finished; then when you are ready to set there are no misfits. Now we are up to the bait stick. It should be no more than nine inches long, and oftentimes shorter will work better. A slotted notch on one end the width of triggers and sharpened at the other is all that is necessary. Then the bait will lie on the foundation of the trap within five or six inches of the front of the trap. Don't put bait too far back under the stone. You lose all the force when it falls.

In building foundations for traps, exercise the utmost caution in making them good and solid. (See how *well* you can do it instead of how *quickly*.) Begin in the fall before the trapping season begins, locate and build your trap, and be sure the top stone is plenty heavy, raise it up and let it fall several times. If it comes together with the bang of a wolf trap and will pinch a hair, so much the better.

An Ohio trapper gave this account to illustrate: "While squirrel shooting one morning in the fall of 1905, I was standing on a ledge where I used to trap for coons, and I happened to remember a trap underneath me. I just thought I would see if it was there. I went down and kicked away the drifted leaves and found it intact and ready for business. When I lifted it up the foundation was as solid as the day I put it there, and that was in the fall of 1890. It was still so strong that it took all the strength I had to set it."

He continued, "Trappers, if you will try one or more of the above described deadfalls for skunks, I think you can tie their pelts about your neck for protection on cold mornings, and none will be the wiser as far as smell goes, provided, however, you put some obstruction to the right and left of the trap so it will compel the skunk to enter directly in front. Carefully adjust the length of the bait stick so the stone will crush the skunk around the area of the heart. I have taken quite a lot of skunk, and very few ever scented where the head and heart were under stone. I always had a preference for the above described traps for many reasons, yet if you live where there is no stone, you must choose another type."

A certain successful deadfall trapper wrote that there is a right and a wrong way to set the deadfall. If you want to make sure of your catch never set your deadfall flat with short triggers shaped like a figure 4, but make long triggers instead and have the weight or choker sit almost upright. Draw the top trigger close to the one that it rests on at the bottom. In this way you have a trap that will be very easy to touch off.

The way that some set their deadfalls the animal can remove bait without being caught, simply because it draws the bait out from under the trap and stands far enough away to be out of danger of being caught. I can take a two hundred pound weight and set a deadfall that will catch a small field mouse, but it would not do to have them knock that easily, for you will get game that is too small to handle.

PORTABLE TRAPS

In describing a portable deadfall, an Indiana trapper wrote as follows: We took a two-by-four of wood about five feet long, then another the same size and length. For upright pieces to hold the main pieces so one would fall square on top of the other, we used two pieces of one-by-three wood, set straight up and down at each end, or about far enough to leave the back end sticking out three inches, and front end or end where the triggers set, six inches.

Nail these one-by-three two on each end as directed above, nail to lower two-by-four piece only, then at back end bore a hole through the two uprights and also upper two-by-four, or the piece that falls, put a bolt through, or a wood pin if the hole in the two-by-four is larger than those through the uprights: then you are ready to raise it up and let it "drop" to see whether it works smoothly or not.

Nail a two-by-four block between the tops of the uprights to keep them from spreading apart. Then it is ready, all except the triggers and string for them to run against. It is portable: you can pick it up and move it anywhere, and only a stake or two is needed to drive down on each side. It should be a small stake, as the little bush in Figure 17 shows.

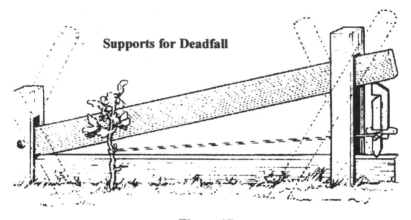

Figure 17

SHEAR TRAP

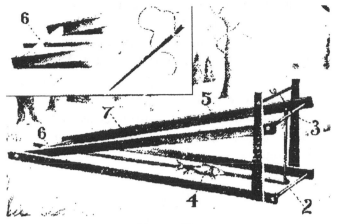

Figure 18

The shear trap is inexpensive, easily made, light-weight to move, and long-lasting. It will catch almost any small animal.

This trap is made as follows: Take four strips of board four feet by four inches long, by three inches wide. Bore a one-inch hole two inches from the end of all four of them. Now make two rounds about thirteen inches long, and put two of the boards on each side of the round.

At the other end put the two outside boards on the other round (see Figure 18). Make one other round fifteen inches long, the same size as the others. Put the two outside boards on it, forming two separate frames at the other end—so the two inside boards can turn on the round to which they are coupled.

Take two strips three inches wide, two feet and six inches long. Bore one inch hole two inches from the top end and put a round broom stick through it seventeen inches long. Fasten all the rounds by wedges or small wooden pins. Stand the two strips last mentioned on the outside of the frame at the end they separate, and make them fast so as to stand perpendicular. For the bait stick take a lathe or a one-half inch board one inch wide. Bore hole as shown (6), and cut notch (2). For trigger any stick eighteen inches long, an inch thick will do: tie string two inches from end and tie other end (1), pass the short end under round from the outside (3), and catch in the notch in the bait lathe (2), put the bait at the other end as shown (4). Put the weight at the top of the slanted piece (5). Cover trap at the end (6) to keep the animal from going through the other side (7). For bait, use fresh fish, muskrat, or bird, and scent with honey or blood.

THE BARREL TRAP

A Northwestern trapper described a barrel trap, which he used for capturing rats. Take any kind of old barrel made of hard wood, or a large tin bucket, and attach a board on one side of the top with a hinge. Let one end of the barrel project out directly over the barrel to within about five to six inches of the other side. Arrange it so that the end of the board not over the barrel is heavier so when the rat tilts down the end in the barrel it will come back into place.

Place a bit of parsnip, apple, or celery near the end of the board over the barrel so when the rat reaches its front feet over on the board it will tilt, sending the rat into the barrel. Bury the barrel near a river or creek to within about two to three inches of the top of the barrel, so there will be from six inches to one foot of water in the barrel. If there is plenty of water in the barrel, most of the rats will be dead by the time you visit your traps. Several may be captured in one night in this kind of trap. (See Figures 19, 20, and 20a.)

Figure 19

This simple trap is great for catching unwanted rats and mi

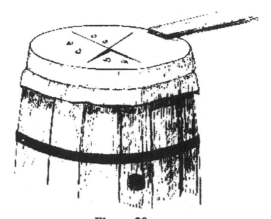

Figure 20

BARREL TRAP

SWIVEL SET

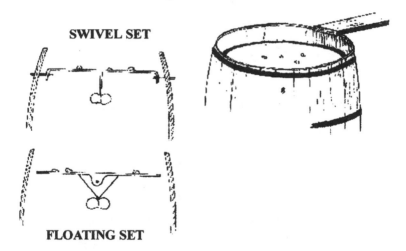

FLOATING SET

Figure 20a

BLOCK TRAP

Saw a small log in blocks from four to six inches long. Bore an inch hole through the center. Drive sharp nails into the blocks so they form a "muzzle" in one end. Fasten your blocks with a piece of wire, and put it in the runway or on a log or anywhere that a coon will see it, and, nine times out of ten, will put his foot into it.

Put stoppers or false bottoms in one end of the block. A piece of corn cob will do. Cut the foot off to get the animal out of this snare. The illustration shows a square block with the hole bored in the side to better show how it should be done, although when set, the hole should be on top. Bait with a piece of fresh rabbit, frog, or anything that coon are fond of, even honey.

Instead of the blocks the auger hole can be bored in a log or root of a tree if a suitable one can be found where coons frequent.

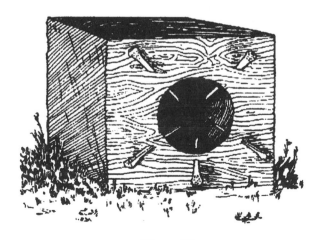

Figure 21
Block Trap
Make sure you check this trap regularly, or you will end up with only a coon leg.

SOME TRIGGERS

The adventurous trapper may want to try some triggers other than the famous "figure 4." One of these triggers is the prop and spindle. The prop and spindle may appear to be too hard to "go off," but it can be set so that it will go off fairly easily. It is not necessary that the trap be set so that the least touch will make it go off. It is best to have the trap set so that mice nibbling at bait will not throw it.

Trappers who have never used deadfalls will, no doubt, find that after they use them a short time and become better acquainted with their construction and operation that they will catch more game than at first. This is only natural as all must learn from experience in general, whether at trapping or anything else.

The prop is a straight piece about seven inches long and about one-half inch in diameter. The spindle, or long trigger, is about the size of the prop, but should be sixteen or eighteen inches long with a prong cut off within two inches of the end to help hold the bait on more securely. See Figures 22 and 23.

Figure 22

Simple Trigger

74

Trigger #1 is a stub driven into the ground with a notch cut in the upper end for the end of the bait. Stick #5 to fit in #3 is another stub driven into the ground for bait stick #5 to rest on top. Number 3 is a stick, one end laid on top of the bait stick outside of stub #2, the other end on top of the lower pole. Number 4 is the prop stick. One end is set on stick #3 about one inch inside the lower pole, the other end underneath the upper pole. The "X" represents the bait. When the bait stick is pulled out of the notch in stub #1, the upper pole comes down and traps the animal.

If you find the bait is caught between the poles you may know the bait is not back in the box far enough. If you find the trap down and the bait and bait stick gone, you may know that the bait is too far back. The animal crawled all the way in before taking the bait and then left the trap without setting off the trigger.

To make a good bait stick, follow these instructions. See the illustration. The trigger sets in the slanting cut in the side. Don't put the bait on the trigger. Put it in the back end of the pen and pin it to the ground. Turn the trigger across the opening slanted slightly in; then the animal is caught by the neck or shoulders. The longer the slot in the trigger, the harder it will trip. Set as straight up as possible.

Make 1 and 2 of hard wood. Saw a block 3 1/2 inches long and split into 3/4-inch squares. Make cuts square with a saw, and split out the part you don't want. Bevel the ends with a hatchet. Make the trigger of green hard wood stick with the bark on.

Cut a tree eight to ten inches in diameter and cut off a length of seven feet. Split the piece open and bury one piece on a level with the earth—split side up—and place the other half on top. Hew off any bumps to make a perfect fit. Then cut out small bushes, and drive them down on each side of the fall, leaving them an inch or two higher than you expect the top log to be when set. Be sure to begin far enough at the back to force the animals to go in at the front. You can try using the "figure 4" triggers and tie the bait to the long trigger.

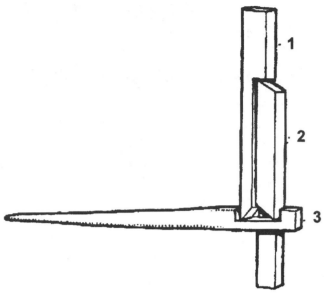

Figure 23

Trip Trigger

The deadfall shown in Figure 24 can be used at dens or in paths where animals travel frequently. When set across the entrance of dens it will catch an animal going in without bait. That is, it will catch an animal going in, as the triggers are so constructed that they can be pushed only toward the bait, as shown in the illustration. If the trap is to be used at dens without bait the regular "figure 4" triggers should be used, but set extending along the log instead of back into the pen. An animal entering will strike the trigger, and down comes the fall.

Figure 24

The trap and the triggers are made as follows: Cut two logs and lay one on the ground. This log should be at least four feet long. Place it firmly on the ground with flat side up. This log need not be as flat as shown in the illustration but should be flattened slightly. Drive two stakes three feet long within a foot or so of one end (8) and (9).

Now come to the other end and drive two more (10) and (11). Stake (10) which is directly opposite from (11) you want to be careful not to split, as one of the triggers rests on it. The fall is now placed in position, that is, the upper log. The end of this is split, and a stake driven in the ground so that the fall will not turn between the stakes but is held firmly. See that the fall will work easily up and down, that the stakes are not so close together that the fall binds, yet it fits snugly.

Cut trip stick (4) and trigger (3), lifting the fall up with one knee and place end of (3) onto (4) slightly, so that a small pressure on (4) will spring the trap. After you have the trap set, spring it to see that it works all right. If the trap works all right and you are setting across the entrance of a den, the pen, of course, is not needed. If you are setting in paths or near dens, drive stakes in a semi-circle as shown in the illustration, but the stakes should stick above the ground about eighteen inches or about as high as the "fall" pole when set. It is a good plan to throw leaves or grass on the stakes.

A small notch (5) should be cut in the upright post (8) for the trip stick to fit in to hold it up to that end. Be careful, however, that this notch is not cut too deep. The bait (6) is placed back in the pen and fastened with wire or a stake driven through it into the ground. The open space over the bait is now covered over, and the entire trap can be made to not look suspicious by cutting brush and throwing it over the trap except in front of the bait. An animal going in for bait steps on or pushes the long stick (4) at one end and at the other (5) off (3) and is usually caught.

TRIP TRIGGER FALL

This is another good trip trigger deadfall. A short log should be laid on the ground and the two stakes driven opposite each other as in the trap just described. These stakes are not shown, so as to afford a better view of the triggers and workings of the trap.

In the illustration (Figure 25) the "fall" pole is weighted, but it is best to have the pole heavy enough and not weighted. The stakes on which the upper or cross piece is nailed should be from twelve to eighteen inches apart. The cross piece need not be heavy, yet should be strong so that the weight of the fall will not bend it.

The pens or enclosures used cannot be covered, as this would interfere with the workings of the triggers. If the pen is sixteen inches or higher, very few animals will climb over to get the bait, but will go in where the trapper intends. If properly made and set, these falls successfully catch the game.

Figure 25

THE TURN TRIGGER DEADFALL

First make a pen in the form of a wigwam (Figure 26), driving stakes well into the ground to keep the animal away from the rear of the trap. It should be open on one side. Place a short log in front of the opening, and at both ends drive stakes to hold it in place and for the long log to work up and down. The top log should be six to eight feet long, according to size of the animal you are trying to trap, and about the same size as the bottom log. Cut a forked stick about one foot long for the bait stick, notching one end and tapering the other as shown in Figure 27. A stick two feet long should then be cut and flattened at both ends.

To set the trap, raise one end of the upper log, and stick one end of the flattened stick under it, resting it upon the top of the stake on the outside of the log. Place the bait stick, point downward, inside the pen upon a chip of wood or rock to keep it from sinking into the ground, and set the flat stick in the notch. When the animal pulls at the bait it turns the bait stake and throws the cross piece out of the notch of the bait stick and lets the top log fall.

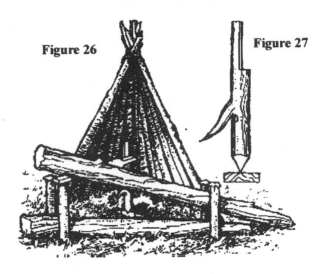

Figure 26

Figure 27

SPRING POLE SNARE

While the deadfall is effective for most animals, there is no one trap that fills all requirements and in all places. Some animals may be wary of deadfalls but can be trapped in spring poles, snares, and steel traps. The spring pole snare is easily and inexpensively constructed. It should be made near dens or where animals travel frequently.

If a small bush is not growing nearby, cut one from another location. (Drive a stake deep into the ground to make a hole, pull it out, and stick the larger end of the cut bush into it.) The numbering of the parts in the diagram (Figure 28) is as follows:

1. bait stick
2. trigger

3. hook made of wire or stout cord
4. stay wire made of wire or cord
5. bait
6. spring pole

By noting carefully the illustration, you can build this trap easily. The size of the bush or spring pole, of course, depends upon what size animals you are trapping. This trap will take small game such as mink, opossum, and skunk, or it can be made large and strong enough to catch mountain lion or black bear. Figures 28a, 28b, and 28c illustrate three additional types of spring pole snares.

Figure 28

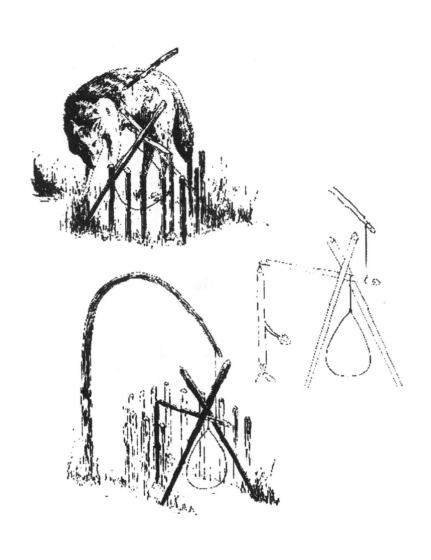

Figure 28a

Another type of spring pole snare

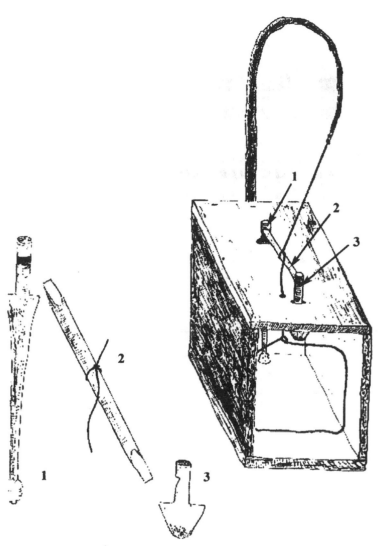

Figure 28b

A spring pole snare set in a box

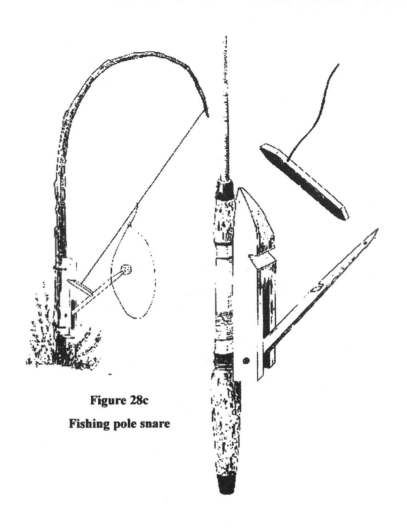

Figure 28c

Fishing pole snare

SMALL GAME SNARE

This snare is made by building a round fence in a place where there are plenty of small trees. Select two about four inches apart for the noose and snare entrance, and another long, springy one for the spring pole six to seven feet long; bend this down and trim it. Have a noose made of limber wire or strong string and a cross piece. Having cut notches in the sides of the trees for the cross piece to fit, set it to spring easily. For snaring rabbits build the fence quite high.

In Figure 29, No. 1 is the noose, No. 2 is the spring pole, No. 3 is the fence, and No. 4 is the bait. This snare can be made any time of the year, while the deadfall can be constructed only when the ground is not frozen.

Figure 29

Small Game Snare

WIRE AND TWINE SNARE

Wire and twine snares work well in cold weather for catching fox and lynx. If properly constructed, they are pretty sure catchers. Figure 30 shows how to set this type.

A-Spring pole

B-Staple

C-Two small nails driven in tree. (Three-inch nail, head en
down, with snare looped at each end with a foot of slac
between.)

D-As soon as the three-inch nail is pulled down, it will sl
past the nail at the top end, when the spring pole w
instantly take up the slack and catch the animal.

E-Slack line or wire

F-Loop should be seven inches in diameter and bottom
loop ten inches from the ground.

  The nails should be driven above the staple so it w
pull straight down to release the snare fastening.

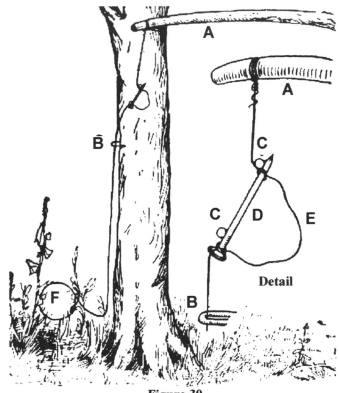

Figure 30

Wire and Twine Snare

86

PATH SET SNARE

This is a successful snare for foxes. (See Figure 31.) A - The snare should be made of rabbit wire, four or five strands twisted together. (For detail, see Figure 32.) It should be long enough to make a loop about seven inches in diameter when set. The bottom side of the snare should be about six inches from the ground.

B - a little stick, sharp at one end to stick in the ground, and split at the other end, to slip the bottom of the snare into, to hold the snare steady.

C - the catch to hold down the spring pole.

D - the stake.

E - the spring pole. Some bend down a sapling for a spring pole, but the best way is to cut and trim a small pole about ten feet long, fasten the big end under a root, and bend it down over a crotch, stake, or small tree. The snare should be set on a summer sheep path, where it goes through the bushes.

The stake might be driven down a foot or more back from the path, where a branch of an evergreen bush would hang over it so as to hide it and a string long enough from the stake or trigger to the snare to rest over the path.

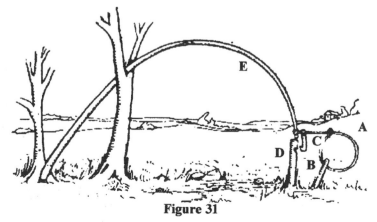

Figure 31

Path Set Snare

87

WIRE SHOWING LOOP.

Figure 32

Detail of Snare Loop

Snares can also be used for animals such as bears. A good sound tamarack tree or other pole fifteen to twenty feet long is used for the tossing. The base end of this must be five or six inches in diameter and the small end about three inches. A tree with a crotch in it is then selected on which to balance the pole. If unable to find such a tree in the proper place, make an artificial fork by crossing two stout, young birch or tamarack, firmly planted in the ground, and tie together the two upper points six to ten inches from the top. The balancing or tossing pole is lodged in this fork so that the part toward the base would outweigh a bear of two or three hundred pounds suspended from the small end.

Next, select a stout little birch or spruce and cut off a section of three to four feet. From this all the branches are removed, except one; the small end is pointed and driven deep into the ground a few inches at one side of the bear road. The snare is made of three twisted strands of eighteen-thread cord line and is firmly tied to the tossing pole. A few dried branches are stuck in the ground on each side of the path, and the pole is depressed so the very end is caught under the twig on the stick driven in the ground. The noose (snare loop) is stiffened by rubbing balsam branches which leave enough gum to make it hold its shape. The bottom of the noose (snare loop) should be about sixteen inches above the road, and the diameter about eleven inches.

88

The noose is kept in the proper position by blades of dry grass looped to it and the ends let into a gash on the sticks at each side. No green branches are used in the hedge around the road, because this would make the bear suspicious. The snare is now complete. The last step is to rub some beaver castor on the trunk of a tree standing near the road, ten to twelve feet from the snare, and to another tree at the same distance on the opposite side of the snare.

Bears are attracted by the smell of the castor and rub themselves against the tree in the same way as a dog rubs on carrion. When finished rubbing on one tree, the bear scents the other and in going to get at the fresh one tries to pass through the snare. It feels the noose tighten about its neck and struggles; this pulls the end of the tossing pole front under the branch trigger, up goes the pole and old Bruin with it.

According to a Massachusetts trapper, a successful way to trap skunks without their scenting is to snare them. Use a spring pole, and if one does not grow nearby, cut one and set it up as firmly as possible about four or five feet from the burrow and to one side. If the ground is frozen, you will have to brace it up with logs or stones or perhaps lash it to a stump or root. When the top of the pole is bent down, it should be caught under the end of a log or rock on the opposite side of the hole so that it can easily be dislodged by an animal, going either in or out of the burrow.

The snare or noose is attached to the spring pole directly over the center of the burrows, and the bottom of the noose should be an inch and a half or two inches from the ground to allow the animal's feet to pass under it and its nose to go through the center. Set the noose as closely over the entrance of the hole as possible, and one or two carefully arranged twigs will keep it in place.

Strong twine is better for the noose than large cord, as the skunk is less likely to notice it. When a skunk passes in or out of the hole, the noose becomes tightened about its neck, and a slight pull releases the spring pole which soon strangles the skunk.

While this may seem an elaborate description of so simple a trap, still, like any other trap, if set in a careless, halfhearted manner, it will meet with indifferent success and, though simple, the snare, with a little thought and ingenuity, can be applied in almost any situation to capture small game.

TRAIL SET SNARE

An Indiana trapper wrote, "Many of the boys have come forth with their particular snares and methods of making them, all of which I believe are good. Most of them, however, require bait, which is one bad feature in certain areas, for it has been my experience that in many localities it is utterly impossible to get animals to take bait. The trail set snare may be used as a blind or set with bait as your trapping grounds, or rather the animals, may require.

"The trail set snare is very inexpensive and so simple any boy can make it. Also, because of the light weight, any man can easily carry one hundred of them and not be too loaded down. First get a strip of iron one-eighth inch thick and three-eighths or one-half inch wide. (See Figure 33.) Cut it in nine-inch lengths, and bend in the shape shown by part B, having drilled a one-fourth inch hole in both ends.

"Next secure some light sheet iron, or heavy tin, cut in pieces 2 3/4 inches by 5 3/4 inches for the pan, and drill a one-fourth-inch hole in the center as shown by part C. It is now a very easy matter to rivet the pan, or part C, to part B. This done, take some 20-penny spikes and cut off the heads as shown by part A.

"Now copper wire, for the loops, can be found on spools at almost any hardware store. It is pliable yet sufficiently strong to hold any of the small furbearers, as it is made in many sizes. Use the copper wire only for the loops. Use ordinary stove pipe wire for the finishing of the snare.

"For a blind set to be placed in the run of the animals, make a double loop, that is, two loops for each snare. Now, take a bunch of these with you and find the runs or follow the ravines and creeks where the animals feed. If you can find a tree in a favorable spot on their runs, take one of your headless spikes and drive it in the base of the tree a few inches from the ground.

"Now take part B with the pan riveted to it and hook bent and over the spike, driving the spike into the tree until the pan is level and until there is just room enough to hook the loop of wire over the head of the spike. (See Figure 34.) Dig out under the pan so it can fall when stepped upon. Then secure a rock or chunk of sufficient weight and fasten to the other end of the wire. Throw this over the limb of the tree, and hook the loop over the head of a spike, having first put part B in place.

"Put one loop on one side of the pan and the other loop on the other side, so an animal coming either way will step upon the pan to its sorrow. This done, drive a staple in the tree over the wire running from spike to limb, which will prevent the animal from being pulled over the limb and escaping.

"Having covered everything up with the natural surroundings and left no signs, you may claim the first furbearer that happens that way and it will be waiting for you. This snare may also be used with the ordinary spring pole by driving a spike into a stake, then the stake into the ground, in which case it is best to make the usual V-shaped pen with stakes or stones, covering them over at the top and setting so the pan will be right in the mouth of the pen and the single loop just between the pan and the bait. In this way the animal treads upon the pan just before it reaches the bait. You will find this snare easily thrown."

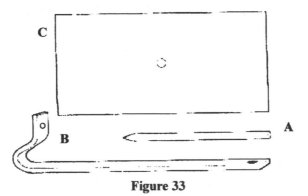

Figure 33

Trip Pan and Plate Assembly

Figure 34

"In many ways the snare is splendid for lynx. In Western Ontario," said a well-known trapper, "where the lynx seldom take bait, they may be taken quite easily in snares set on snowshoe trails." Figures 35 and 36 show wire snares set on such a trail.

Set the snare in the following manner: Having found a suitable place along the edge of some swamp or alder thicket, cut a spruce or balsam tree, about ten to twelve feet long, and throw it across the trail. Press the tree down until the stem of the tree is about twenty inches above the trail, and make an opening in the trail by cutting a few of the limbs away on the underside of the trail. Then set a couple of stakes on each side so as to leave the opening about ten inches wide. Hang the snare between these stakes and directly under the stem of the tree.

The snare should be about nine inches in diameter and should be fastened securely to the tree. It should also be fastened lightly to the stakes on either side, so it will not spring out of shape. The best way is to make a little split in the side of each stake, and fasten the snare with a very small twig stuck in the split stake.

The snares can be made of rabbit wire, about four or five piles thick, twisted. Some trappers prefer to use a cord. The dark colored codfish line is best, and it is best to use a spring pole snare. Figure 37 shows the method of tying and fastening to the stakes. It will be seen that when the lynx passes its head through the snare it needs only to give a slight pull to open the slip knot and release the spring pole.

To prevent the rabbits from biting a cord snare, rub it well with the dropping of the lynx or fox. Also, never use any green wood other than spruce or balsam, as any fresh green wood is sure to attract the rabbits. You may also put a small piece of beaver castor along the trail on each side of the snare, and you will be more sure of attracting lynx, as beaver castor is very appealing to these big cats.

Figure 35

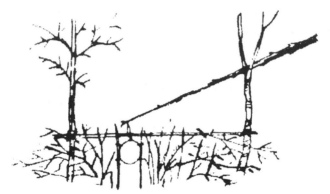

Figure 36

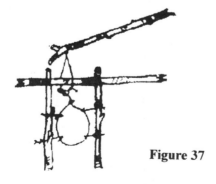

Figure 37

94

Below is another another spring pole snare, described by a Colorado trapper. It is made like the preceding one except for the trigger. This one is to be used on a runway without any bait. Figure 38 shows the trigger in the runway. A is the trip stick; B, the stay crotch; C, the trigger; D, the loop; E, the pathway, and F, the stay wire.

The animal in coming on down the path (E) passes its body or neck through the loop made of stout, soft insulated wire (D) ; in passing it steps on the trip stick (A) which settles with the animal's weight, releasing the trigger (C) which in turn releases the stay wire (F) and jerks the loop (D) around the animal. The spring pole onto which the stay wire is attached lifts the animal into the air, choking it to death and placing it out of reach of other animals that would otherwise destroy the fur. A small notch cut in the stay crotch where the end of the trip stick rests will ensure that the trigger will be released. This will hold the trip stick firm at the end, allowing it to move only at the end where the animal steps.

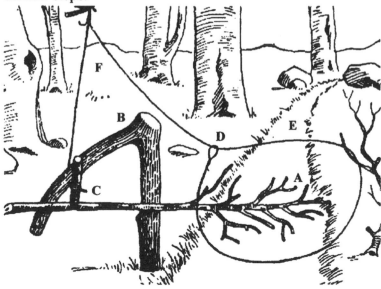

Figure 38

SELF-LOCKING SNARES

Self-locking snares are very inexpensive and are easily made. Figures 39 and 40 illustrate two types of self-locking snares. The first self-locking snare (Figure 39) is attached to a wooden stake at the entrance of a den.

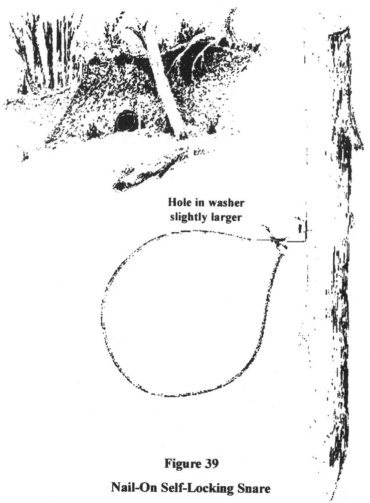

Hole in washer
slightly larger

Figure 39

Nail-On Self-Locking Snare

Snares are the lightest and least expensive, most effective trap known to man. They are perfect for survival backpack trips.

The second self-locking snare (Figure 40) is placed in the runway of small furbearers. In the illustration, a tree root bridges a portion of the runway. It may be necessary to close off the rest of the runway by driving several poles into the ground. This forces the small furbearer to go through the portion of the runway where the snare is located. The detailed close-up indicates how the self-locking snare would be attached to the tree root in Figure 40.

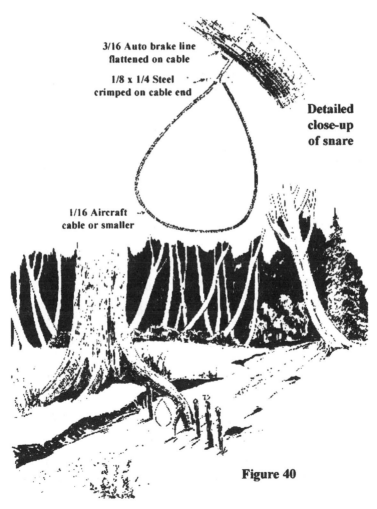

3/16 Auto brake line
flattened on cable

1/8 x 1/4 Steel
crimped on cable end

Detailed close-up of snare

1/16 Aircraft
cable or smaller

Figure 40

BOX TRAPS

This trap is put to various uses. The beginner usually has one or two with which he traps for rabbits. The animal is not injured, which is often the case when shot or caught by dogs. Rabbits caught in box traps are therefore the best for eating. The trapper who wants to secure furbearers alive to sell to parks or menageries, or to start a "fur ranch" usually uses the box trap.

The size of the box trap for rabbits is about thirty inches long by five inches wide and six inches high. The boards can be of any kind, but pine and poplar are used often because they are lightweight. The boards need only be a half inch thick. You will need four pieces thirty inches long; two of these for the sides should be six inches wide; the other two for top and bottom should be five inches. These pieces should be nailed on the top and bottom of the sides. This will make the inside of the trap six inches high by four inches wide. It is best to make the trap narrow so the trapped animal cannot turn around.

In one end of the trap, place wires or small iron rods (see Figure 41). These should be about an inch apart. Construct the door out of wire at the other end. The bottom of the door should strike about eight inches inside. An animal pushing against the door, from the outside, raises it, but once on the inside the more the animal pushes against the door, the tighter the trap becomes.

The trap can be set at holes where game is known to be, or it can be baited and placed where game frequents. If bait is used place a little prop under the door, and place the bait back in the trap a foot or more. Bait to use, of course, depends upon what you intend to trap.

The trap described is about the right size for the common rabbit and mink. For skunk and opossum a trap a little larger will be required.

For mink and other animals that are gnawers, visit the traps daily, because the animals may gnaw and escape. If impossible to visit the traps daily, line them with tin.

In many places these traps, with a door at each end, are used for catching muskrats. They are set in their dens under water and either tied or weighted down. The muskrats are caught either going in or leaving.

In making these traps the beginner is apt to make them too wide, so the animal can turn inside them. This is a mistake, for it gives the game more freedom and room to gnaw itself free.

If the trap is made properly, the animal simply goes in and is there until the trapper comes along and removes the game. Skunks can be drowned when caught in this trap without scenting if the trapper knows how to go about it.

The trap should be handled carefully. Take to water sufficiently deep to cover the trap and slowly sink. Then either weight the trap or hold down until the animal is drowned.

The animal, of course, could gnaw out, but will drown before it has time to accomplish this. Where muskrats are numerous, several rats are often taken in a night. Traps of this kind can be used to best advantage in lakes and ponds where the height of the stream does not vary much. If they are set along creeks and rivers, fasten them securely or take them up before heavy rains, as they are almost sure to be washed away.

The box trap is a humane trap if visited daily. It is rather cumbersome to carry around, and few trappers want many, yet under certain conditions it is very useful. It can be made during idle time. For mink and other shy animals, the trap should be handled as little as possible. It should be made of old boards or at least avoid all appearances of newness.

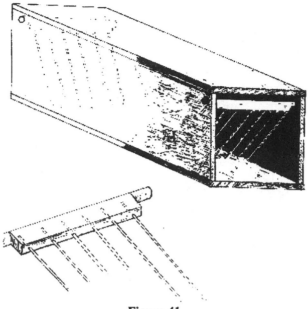

Figure 41

A good muskrat box trap is worth its weight in gold. Try this one.

First take four boards thirty-six inches long and nail them together, leaving both ends open. Next construct a small gate for each end, with a square piece of wood and a few stiff wires. Position each gate to pivot inside each opening so as to work freely and fall easily when raised. Fasten the bait inside the center of the box. The animal in quest of the bait finds an easy entrance, as the wires lift at slight pressure, but the exit after the gate has closed is so difficult that escape is almost beyond question. To ensure further strength it is advisable to connect the lower ends of the wires by a crosspiece of fine wire twisted about each. You can catch two and three in this trap on a good night. Set in two or three inches of water where muskrats frequent. For skunks, set in skunk dens.

100

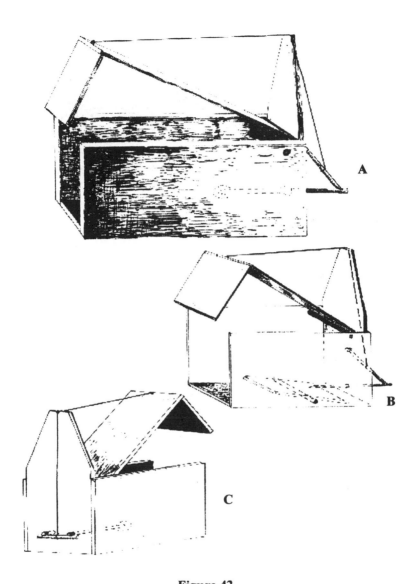

Figure 42

Common Box Trap

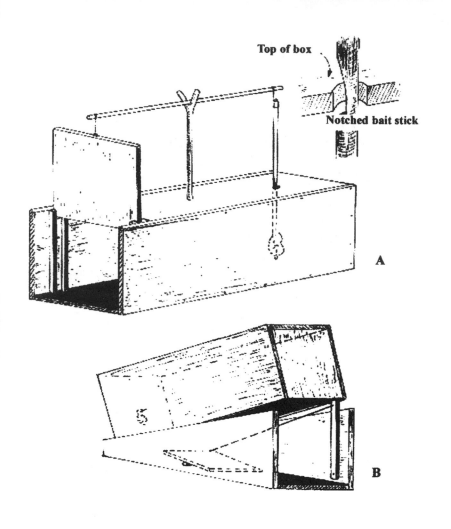

Top of box

Notched bait stick

A

B

Figure 43

Another Box Trap

102

THE COOP TRAP

This trap is used with great success for catching wild turkey, pheasants, quail, and other feathered game. In some states the law forbids the use of this and similar traps. Find out the laws of the state in which you plan to trap.

The trap is built like an ordinary rail pen. In fact, some use small rails when constructing this trap for wild turkey, while others build of small straight poles. The pen is usually six feet or more square and about three high. The "coop" is stronger if drawn in from bottom to top (see Figure 44). The top must be covered and weighted.

A ditch is now dug about a foot wide. This ditch should begin about three feet from the coop and lead within. Corn or other grain is scattered on the outside and in the trench leading into the coop. On the inside considerable feed should be scattered in the leaves and small twigs.

The turkeys once on the inside will eat the grain and scratch among the leaves which generally partly fill the trench, and as the birds are usually looking up when not eating, they do not think of the trench through which they entered.

The same trap will catch quail, but of course is built much smaller. About three feet square and a foot high is sufficient. Some trappers have built quail coops out of cornstalks and report catches.

The quail coop should have the ditch leading to the inside the same as described for turkey. Of course, the ditch should be much smaller—only large enough for one bird to enter at a time. On the inside of the coop it is a good idea to lay a board six inches or wider over the ditch. The bait should be wheat or other small grain or seeds that the birds like. Scatter thinly on the outside and in the trench, but on the inside place more liberally. Chaff or leaves should be placed on the inside so the birds in scratching for the grain will partly fill up the hole through which they came.

Quail, turkey, and other feathered game, once inside the trap and after eating the bait, never think of going down into the ditch and out, but walk around and around the coop looking through the chinks and trying to escape.

The largest catches are made by baiting where the birds frequent for some days or even weeks before trying to make a catch. It is well to make the coops long in advance so the birds, especially wild turkey, will be accustomed to them.

Figure 44

WHERE TO BUILD

In determining where to set deadfalls or locate snares, if you have trapped before, keep in mind the dens where in previous winters you have caught fur-bearing animals, or their tracks have often been seen in the snow or mud. Build your traps and construct snares at or near such places.

The location, of course, depends largely upon what kind of game you are trying to catch. If mink or coon, there is no better place than along streams where there are dens. If there should be a small branch leading off from the main stream, the mouth of this is often an excellent place to put a trap. It should not be too near the water, as a rise would damage or perhaps float off at least part of your trap. Sometimes farther up this small stream there may be bluffs and rocks; at such places, if there are dens, build deadfalls there. If there are several dens, and the bluff extends along several hundred feet, it perhaps will pay to build two or three traps here.

In cleared fields, woods, or thickets, where skunks are found, anywhere there are dens you can construct a trap. While, as a rule, the thinly settled districts are the best trapping sections, skunk, muskrat, and red fox are found in greatest numbers in settled sections, while opossum, raccoon, and mink are found in fairly well settled districts. It is therefore not necessary that you go into the wilderness to make fairly good catches.

While the trapper in the wilderness has the advantage of no one disturbing his deadfalls, he also has disadvantages. The trapper who means business need not go hundreds of miles away, but if he will build a line of traps along some stream where there are mink, or in the thickets and along rocky bluffs for skunk, raccoon, opossum, and other animals, he will be surprised at his results.

Note: In populated areas, please be careful to set your traps where domestic animals and people are not likely to be hurt. The joy of trapping game could quickly become remorse if the animal turns out to be a neighbor's pet.

In some sections land owners may not allow trapping, but usually they will, especially if you take the time to ask before you begin building or setting your traps.

Scattering your traps over a large territory gives you a better chance of making good catches, because most animals travel quite a distance from night to night. You may have traps at some stream that is eight or ten miles from your home, and a mink may come along that does most of its seeking for food miles farther up or downstream, nearer, perhaps, where it was raised. Thus by going only ten miles away you may catch animals that really live twenty miles away. Sometimes animals continue their travels from one stream to another.

If you are an expert trapper you can very easily detect furbearers, if you are in a good locality, especially in the fall—September and October. These are the two months when the most prospecting is done. Walking along streams at this season, you can plainly see tracks, and in the forest you can see signs near dens, such as hair, bones, and dung. Often you will come upon signs where a bird has been devoured and you know that some animal has been in the area. Old trappers readily detect all these signs, and new ones can learn by experience.

It is not absolutely necessary to build traps at or near dens. Some years ago, a trapper in southern Ohio came upon a deadfall built near a small stream that ran through a woods. He looked around for dens but saw none. Why this trap had been built there was a puzzle to him. One day, he happened upon the owner of the trap and asked him what he expected to catch in that trap.

In reply the owner pointed to a bush a few yards away in which hung the carcasses of two opossum and one coon caught in the trap. While there were no dens near, it was a favorite place for animals to cross or else they came there for water. With this same trap the old trapper caught two or three animals each winter, while other traps near dens caught fewer animals. Keep your eyes open for signs, and you will learn where to build traps and set snares sooner or later.

THE PROPER BAIT

Bait is sometimes difficult to get, but usually the trapper will get enough with his gun and steel traps to keep his line of deadfalls well baited, without difficulty. In trapping, all animals caught after the pelt is taken off should be hung so other animals cannot reach them but will visit your traps.

There are two purposes in hanging up bait: First, other animals coming along are likely to eat them and not visit your deadfall; second, should you run out of bait you can cut a piece from the animal hanging up, bait your trap, and go to the next. While bait of this kind is not recommended, sometimes it can be a last resort. Fresh bait is preferable, yet the trapper cannot always get what he knows is best and consequently must do the next best. Perhaps by his next visit he will have bait in abundance.

Some trappers have used a piece of skunk, opossum, muskrat, or coon that had been caught some weeks before and hung up in a sapling where it froze. On the next visit the trap baited with skunk contained a skunk. This shows that when an animal is very hungry it is not very particular what it eats.

In the early fall while food of all kinds is easy to find, any animal is harder to entice to bait, and at this season bait should be fresh if the trapper expects to make profitable catches.

The trapper should always carry a gun, pistol, or good revolver to help kill game to supply bait for his traps. Steel traps set along the line will also help to keep the supply of bait up at all times. If you are successful in securing a great deal of bait, more than will be used on that round, you will find it an excellent idea to leave some at certain places where it can be secured on the next round should it be needed.

Bait may consist of any tough bit of meat, but rabbit is an excellent bait. Quail or almost any bird is good. Chicken also makes good bait. Squirrel is satisfactory. For mink, fish is excellent. Frogs and muskrat can also be used. Remember that the fresher and bloodier the bait, the better—animals will scent it much more quickly. They are also fonder of fresh bait than that which has been killed for days, or weeks, as the case may be.

In baiting it is important to see that the bait is attached securely. It is a good idea to tie it on with strong thread or small cord. The amount of bait to put on a single trap is not important. Most trappers use a rabbit in baiting ten traps or fewer; the head makes bait for one trap, each foreleg another, the back about three and each hind leg one, although each hind leg can be cut to make bait for two traps.

The spindle or trigger is run thru the bait and should be fastened on the trigger near the end. If the bait is not on securely and the trap is hard to get off, the animal may devour bait and the trap may not fall. If the trigger is only sticking loosely in the bait, it is easy for an animal to steal the bait. Usually the observing trapper knows these things and is on his guard, but for those who are using deadfalls for the first time, more explicit explanation is necessary.

The bait should extend back into the pen about a foot, and the pen should be so constructed that the bait touches only on the trigger. To eat the bait, the animal usually stands with its forefeet upon the under pole, or just over it. If its gnawing at the bait twists the trigger off the upright prop, the animal will be caught across the back. An animal standing in the position just described will naturally pull down somewhat on the bait and in its eagerness to get the bait pull and twist the spindle, or trigger, off the upright prop.

It is a good idea to try the trigger. That is, place the triggers under the fall just the same as you would if they were baited and you were going to set the trap. By doing this you will find out about how you want to set the triggers so that they will work properly. There is much involved in learning how traps work. Study carefully, and you will soon learn to be a successful trapper.

FALSE ALARMS

If you find that your traps are "down" each time you visit them and the bait gone, the pen is perhaps too large, and the animal, if a small one like a mink, is going inside to devour bait. Animals usually stand with forefeet upon the lower log and reach into the pen after the bait, but at times they have been known to go inside. In this case the animal is not in as much danger as when the "fall" comes down and the animal is not under it. If such is the case, that is, the animal entirely inside the pen, the trigger will be caught under the fall and the trapper knows that whatever is molesting his trap is doing so from the inside. All that the trapper has to do is make the pen smaller. This can be done by placing small stones or chunks on the inside of the pen or by driving stakes on the inside. By doing this the outside appearance is not changed.

If, on the other hand, the trigger, that is the long one or spindle, not the short prop, is pulled out each time and often carried several feet, the trap is set too hard to "fall" and should be set more easily. If the prop, or upright piece, is cut squarely across the top, round off the edges with a knife so that the trigger will slip off more easily. Again the pen may be torn down and the animal may take bait from the rear. Here is where it pays to build sturdy traps. In such cases rebuild the pen, making it stronger. Should it be torn down on subsequent visits, the culprit is perhaps a fox.

Of course, if the pen has been torn down by some trapper or passing hunter, you can readily detect that by the manner in which it has been done. If the trapper is satisfied that it is an animal that is doing the mischief, he wants to plan carefully, and if he is an expert trapper, a steel trap or two will come into good play, and the animal will be caught in the steel trap. The pen will not be torn down again.

When traps are down, note carefully the condition they are in; see that the "fall" fits on the lower pole closely. When building traps, it is important that the fall fits snugly on the lower or under pole.

If a snare or spring pole is up but nothing caught, simply reset. Should many snares be "thrown" and no catches, try to locate the trouble at once. The noose is probably too large or small or made of too limber or too stiff string or wire, or maybe it is too securely fastened. When resetting, note all these factors carefully, and experience will sooner or later enable you to set just right to make a catch. If a certain snare is bothered continually, it will do no harm to set a steel trap where you think chances best of taking the animal. It matters little to the trapper how the animal is caught, as long as he gets the pelt.

In using the trip triggers with bait, the trapper should fasten the bait by either driving a peg through it and into the ground or tying. In most instances the animal will throw the trap before getting to the bait, but it is well to take this precaution in case, for any reason, the animal should not step on the trip trigger at first.

Sometimes a small animal may jump over the trip trigger in order to get the bait and in its endeavor to get bait will strike the trigger. The animal does not know that the trigger is dangerous, but now and then either steps or jumps over. Generally it steps on the trigger, for if the trapper has done a good job, the bait and trigger are so placed that the animal thinks the trip trigger is the place to put its foot.

In using the trigger without bait, the trigger is so arranged that the animal rubs or steps on the trigger when entering or leaving the pen or, if at a trail or runway, when passing along.

WHEN TO TRAP

The proper season to begin trapping is when cold weather comes. The rule for trappers to follow is to put off trapping in the fall until nights are frosty and the ground freezes. The fall is when furs are prime. The old saying that fur is good any month that has an "r" in its name applies only in the North. Even in the North, September is too early to begin for prized furs, such as fox and coyotes. Less valuable furs, such as muskrat, skunk, and raccoon, can be caught just about anytime. April is the last month with an "r." In most sections muskrat, bear, beaver, badger, and otter are good all through April, but other animals begin shedding weeks before.

Generally speaking in Canada and the more northern states trappers can begin about November 1 and should cease March 1, with the exception of water animals, bear, and badger, which may be trapped a month later. In the central and southern states trappers should not begin as early and should stop in the spring from one to four weeks earlier—depending upon how far south they are located.

The skunk is the first animal to become prime, then the coon, marten, fisher, mink, and fox, but the latter does not become strictly prime until after a few days of snow, reported an old Maine trapper. Rats and beaver are late in priming as well as otter and mink, and though the mink is not strictly a land animal, it becomes prime about with the later land animals. The bear, which is strictly a land animal, is not in good fur until snow comes and not strictly prime until February or March.

With the first frosts and cool days many trappers begin setting and baiting their traps. Most trappers know that it is easier to catch certain kinds of furbearing animals early in the season, and for this reason trapping in most localities is done too early in the season.

In the latitude of southern Ohio, Indiana, and Illinois, skunk caught in the month of October are graded back from one to three grades (and even sometimes into trash), whereas if they were not caught until November 15, their classification would have been much higher. The same is true of opossum, mink, muskrat, coon, and fox.

That the weather has much to do with the priming of furs and pelts there is no question. If the fall is colder than usual the furs will become prime sooner, while if the freezing weather comes later the pelts will be later in priming.

In the areas where weasels turn white (then called ermine by many), trappers have a good guide. When weasels become white they are prime, and so are most other land animals. In fact, some are fairly good a week or two before.

When a pelt is put on the stretcher and becomes blue in a few days it is far from prime and will grade no better than No. 2. If the pelt turns black the chances are that the pelt will grade No. 3 or 4. In the case of mink, when dark spots only appear on the pelt, it is not quite prime.

Trappers and hunters should remember that no pelt is prime, or No. 1, when it turns the least blue. Opossum skins seldom turn blue even if caught early, but most other skins do.

A WINTER'S NIGHT IN THE WOODS WITHOUT BLANKETS

Traveling with an old trapper and his dog Ginger

When you find yourself too far from camp to make it before dark, well, there's no sense in pushing on any further; we wouldn't be able to reach camp tonight, anyhow. I wouldn't say that spending a night under the winter stars without blankets is something we'd do by choice, but I reckon we can make ourselves and the dog comfortable enough so we can get a few hours' sleep, anyway.

Trouble was, I didn't figure that bobcat would give us such a long chase. But seeing as you got a right prime hide out of it and I got the fun of watching old Ginger dog work—as pretty a job of trailing by a hound as I ever saw— well, I'm not grumbling about a night in the open. We have our belt axes, dry matches, and some leftover grub, so we ought to make out pretty fair.

We'd better get busy now, while there's still a mite of daylight. Here's as good a place as any I've seen in the last half hour—over on the lee side of that big rock. See, she's got a flat face going up almost straight, and that smaller rock leaning against her makes about a right angle, something like two sides of a box. Snow's drifted in there some, but it'll be worth the extra shoveling. That big beech blow-down will give us firewood enough, and that clump of balsam fir over by the brook is nice and handy.

Use one of your snowshoes for a shovel, and we'll dig a hole clear down to the ground and get all the snow away from the face of the rock; about nine feet by five is the right size, I guess. Ah, that's good; rocky bottom holds the heat better. Now if you'll start on the beech—only fairly thick pieces cut to about six-foot lengths—I'll finish the hole. Notice that I'm making it about nine feet alongside this big rock, and I'm digging out the corner where the smaller rock makes an angle.

Well, that's quick work. Drop the wood right in the hole, and I'll start a fire under it. There she goes! Now I'll give you a hand on the woodpile. Yes, dump it all right on the fire. The bigger the better. Listen to her roar! Now for the fir boughs. Cut only the green stuff, lopping off the big boughs. We can use 'em. Better let them lie as they fall, for it'll soon be too dark in that thick growth to use an axe without danger of an accident, and we'll need plenty of boughs.

Whew! That's warm work. Reckon that'll do us. We'll drag them right up to the edge of the fire. Wow, she's hot; we're going to have a nice bed of coals, and the rocky ground and the side of that boulder are going to hold the heat for a long time.

While we're waiting for the fire to burn down, we might as well get that grub ready, and the water boiling for tea. We'll use the near edge of the fire. If you'll do that, I'll cut a ten- or twelve-foot pole that we're going to need.

That's done. Tea ready? Good thing I always bring some emergency rations on these outings. I don't mind saying I'm a little hungry. How about you? Jerky tastes good, and here we have three or four biscuits apiece, and a couple of chocolate bars. Well, guess we'll last till we reach camp.

There, now, fire's done its job. We'll poke all the unburned pieces down against the face of the smaller rock; we're going to keep a little fire going there. Now for the fir boughs, right on the dying coals. Pile 'em on thick. They won't burn; they've got more or less snow on 'em and they're green. That's about enough.

Now I'll lay the pole I cut lengthwise over the hole, resting it on the snow pile down at this end and on the smaller rock at the other end. The pole ought to just touch the fir boughs before we get our weight on them. Now we'll stand the rest of the boughs, butts down, against the pole so

116

that we'll have a roof over our heads, and our shelter's all ready.

Just crawl in with me under the pole and find a comfortable spot. Come in here, Ginger! Smoke bother you? It won't be so bad in a little while. Smells good, doesn't it? Feel that warm glow from the rock. Now we'll try to snatch a few hours' snooze. I'll keep the little fire going down there by our feet. It's a cold night, but we're warm enough, and by daylight we'll be rested for that twelve-mile shuffle back to camp.

ALL ABOUT
THE
OUTDOORS

A CAMP LANTERN

If you're caught out unexpectedly and can't make it back to camp, try this kind of lantern. You can make it about as quickly as a squirrel can climb a tree. Grab an empty tin can. Cut an "X" in the side with a metal punch or with the tip of your hunting knife, and push in the four points to make a hole to insert a candle. Cut two smaller holes opposite the candle hole. Fasten a wire handle through the two little holes opposite the candle hole. Thrust a candle inside the can, strike a match, and there you are! The little candle flame in the tin can will throw a long ray of brilliance on a dark night. It's almost as good as a flashlight. As the candle burns down, push it up.

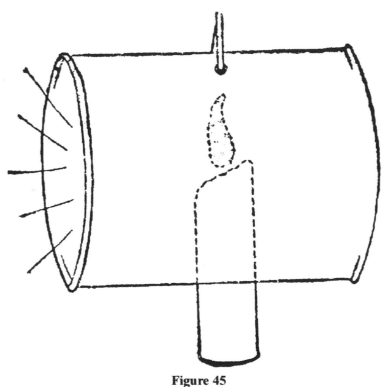

Figure 45
Camp Lantern
120

HOW TO FIND YOUR WAY BY THE STARS

It is very important that those who frequent the forest should be sufficiently familiar with the stars to be able to tell their way by them. Often a compass is lost or damaged or there is not enough light to see the landmarks. At such a time a knowledge of how to find the North Star (also called Polaris or the polestar) is invaluable, for to the experienced woodsman, a glimpse of this star is equivalent to consulting a compass. Although not very bright, the North Star is really the most important of the stars we see, because it marks the North at all times and is fixed in its place, while all the other stars seem to swing around it once every twenty-four hours.

Figure 46
NORTH HORIZON

The Big Dipper, or Great Bear, is well known to most American youngsters because of the size, peculiar shape, and brilliancy of this group, and the fact that it never sets in this latitude. This constellation always points out the North Star, which is approximately in a line with the stars (Alpha and Beta) which form the outside of the Dipper at a distance about three and a half times as great as the space separating these two stars. If the imaginary line between Alpha and Beta and the North Star is continued about the same distance beyond the North Star, it will meet Cassiopeia, five stars in the shape of a "W," which, like the Great Bear, is always seen in the northern hemisphere. With these directions it should always be easy to locate the North Star.

YOU'RE LOST! NOW WHAT?

Told by Deep River Jim

If you talk with woodsmen and get the straight scoop, you'll find there's mighty few who won't be willing to tell you that, on occasion they've got all turned around and didn't know north from a chickadee. It hurts a man's pride to admit he's lost. Davy Crockett once said, "I've never been lost, but I was confused for three weeks one time." The fellows who haven't been lost haven't had such a heap of experience or haven't been off the beaten trail farther than you could throw a rock. The old pioneers themselves often got lost and used their common sense and woods sense in getting out. Follow this advice, and you may save your hide.

Now, I want to tell you about that last experience of mine and give you some help on what to do if it happens to you. Seems as if a lot of fellows think that the north side of all trees everywhere is always covered with moss as thick as fur on the back of an old black bear and that the tops of all trees slant sharply to the east or the west. But, say, when you're lost you usually have to do a lot more than look for moss and gaze at the tops of trees. Just for instance, suppose you get tangled up on a pitch black night. Believe me, you're not going to get very far feeling around for moss or doing any tree gazing.

Well, now, let's get started about that last time I was deep in the woods and didn't know this way from that. It was night, too, and just about as black as a bat's cave.

I went off late in the afternoon from camp with a pal of mine trout fishing, and we reached the stream just a little before sunset on a cloudy afternoon. At the place where we started fishing, the brook crossed a wooded road and emptied into a small lake. For a couple of hours we fished upstream and had a pretty good blessing from the Lord's storehouse of provision. The tackle bag slung across my shoulder was getting heavier as the dusk grew deeper. When we were a couple of miles up above the lake, it was getting very dark. Pretty soon there wasn't enough light to see the pools. So I yelled to Bill, "We'd better quit this," and of course he agreed, and we stood on the side of the brook and debated about what we should do. I said, "Let's walk along the brook upstream until we come to the log bridge."

That old wooded road made a wide curve from the lake up toward the headwaters of the brook and crossed the stream again. So there were several square miles of wilderness shaped something like a melon with the wooded road forming about half the boundary and the brook the other half.

Well, Bill countered my proposal by suggesting that instead of walking all the way up the brook to the bridge, we cut straight through the woods and hit the road lower down. He had been in there before and said he could do it, and I, kind of wondering whether he could or not, said, "Okay. Let's go."

By that time maybe you could have seen a bull moose if he'd been standing ten feet away, and maybe you couldn't, and we hadn't gone a quarter of a mile before Bill said, "Guess we'd better turn around, Jim, and find that brook."

Now here's something about getting lost you always want to remember: You get lost in the first ten minutes—always. You know what happened next. We couldn't find that brook! It just seemed to have gone off somewhere else, out of that neck of the woods. One reason why we couldn't find it, I reckon, was that every time I led the way, Bill said I kept turning to the left, and every time he led the way, I said he kept turning to the right, taking us in a circle.

After about half an hour—and by that time you couldn't have seen the bull moose unless he butted you—

we laughed and admitted to each other that we were a couple of lost guys and we ought to be ashamed of it. Of course, being in a piece of timber completely surrounded by a road and a stream, we weren't in any bad fix, and you might not think there was any special danger, but, boys, there's always danger when you get lost in the woods! The particular danger that night was from falling and breaking a leg—or something worse. It had started to rain and everything was wet and slippery, and I'm not exaggerating a mite when I say there were about ten thousand bog holes and twice as many blown down trees and timber tangles in those few square miles of black forest.

Right here I want to tell you the first rule to follow if you get lost, especially at night and when you're alone: Stop and make camp as soon as you know you're lost. Say to those legs of yours, "Quit moving. You've got me all twisted up and I'm going to give you a rest."

If you've never been lost you haven't any idea what a nameless dread comes over you, especially when you're alone. It scares you from your head to your big toe, and the way men lose their lives is by starting off in a panic, running—going and going and going, keeping it up to the point of exhaustion, and all the time getting deeper and deeper into the wilderness and then probably they fall and break a leg.

You'll read in the newspapers every now and then about people getting lost, and some of them never come out, and you can just put it down in your notebook that the ones who stay there forever are the ones who go into a panic and run wild. So the first rule is: Stay calm—and stop moving if you don't know the general lay of the land.

On this particular night I'm telling you about, Bill and I knew that we had to be mighty careful, but we knew there wasn't any harm in moving around, so long as we didn't get hurt, because we knew that if we could keep

125

going in a straight line we'd hit either the brook or the wood road. That was the problem—how to go straight.

Now, you'll ask, "Where was your compass?" And you'll have a good laugh when I tell you it was back in camp! I never thought we'd need it, just going off on a trout fishing expedition. But just suppose we had had a compass. How would we have used it? Not a dry match in any of our pockets. No flashlight. Believe me, that taught me a lesson, never to go into the woods anywhere without a waterproof match box, a rule which I have never broken since.

Now just stop and think what you would have done in those circumstances. Then I'll tell you how Bill and I went at it.

First of all we stood still and talked things over. Remember that. And take note also that if we had not known the general lay of the land we would have camped right there for the night. But we said to each other that here was a good chance to try out some methods. What we needed was a guide to keep us in a straight line. The first guide we tried was light in the sky. It was so dark down there under the trees in that tangle of undergrowth that we could see no difference of light in any direction. However, we knew that the sky in the west should still be lighter than the horizon in an hour or so, although it would be hidden by the rain clouds.

So we shinned a couple of trees, and I never knew before what a good shinner I am! The tree I picked was wet and slippery like all the others, but I went up it like a sailor climbing a greased pole, and finally I got high enough so that I thought I could make out a lighter area of sky in one direction and a slightly lighter area in another direction. Bill did the same thing. That gave us a hint, but when we got down on the ground again we had to go along by memory

126

and guesswork, and, after shinning so many trees that we felt like a pair of monkeys, we decided to try another method—that of lining up trees.

It's easy in daylight to keep straight. You line up three trees ahead of you. Go to the first, to the second, to the third; then pick out three more which are ahead of you and in line with the one by which you stand and the second one behind you; then you go ahead again.

On a black night in a dense forest that method doesn't work. You may succeed in making out the tops of trees ahead of you when you look up toward the sky, but as soon as you move ten steps you cannot be sure which trees you picked out. Everything is vague; outlines of treetops are indistinct, and you very quickly realize that it just isn't going to work.

Well, we had another trick up our sleeves—the sound method. Bill stood still, and I went ahead yelling back to him every few steps. He would shout to me to turn a little to the right or a little to the left to keep me on a straight course. Finally, when I had gone so far that I could barely hear him, I yelled for him to come up, and along he came, following my occasional shouts. Then he would go ahead while I stayed behind and shouted directions. The great difficulty in that method is to continue your relaying in a straight line from the original starting point. If you don't watch out, you'll zigzag and possibly even come around in a complete circle as you would in following the edges of an octagon.

In all probability, Bill and I would have worked our way out by this sound method, but we were right in the midst of it when along came a bit of unexpected help. Nothing less than a glint of moonlight through the dark trees, just a tiny gleam as the moon slipped a glance earthward through the clouds. That instantly gave us our points of the compass, east, west, north, south, and we decided immediately to go east. Things were easy after that, for about every two or three minutes we caught another glimpse of that obliging moon, and within the hour we stepped out on the wooded road and left the swamp and the bogholes, the blowdowns, and the dense thickets behind us.

Although we were dripping wet from head to foot and more or less scratched up from shinning those trees and scrambling over the blowdowns, and had been through a terrifically tiring ordeal, we stopped right there and laughed. But you can take it from me that it wouldn't have been any laughing matter if a person in that piece of wilderness had lost his head and run wild.

We tramped back to camp, changed our wet clothes, got some hot food, and felt as good as ever—and pretty contented to roll up in our warm blankets instead of spending the night on some water-soaked knoll waiting for daylight.

Now of course circumstances vary a heap. If you're lost when you can see the sun at evening or the strong glow of the sky from the sun after it has set, you know where west is. Facing the west you know that when you stretch your arms out wide, your right hand points to the north, your left hand points to the south, and your back is to the east. The same with the setting moon, and of course the reverse when you face the rising sun or the rising moon. It is well to remember, however, that there is a variation with the seasons of the year, the moon swinging more to the south in summer, for example. On a starlit night it's easy to get your points of compass from the North Star, and finding the North Star is simple enough. Every woodsman knows that the two stars forming the side of the Big Dipper away from the handle point straight up toward the North Star.

Then knowing the lay of the land is mighty important. In unfamiliar country you should never be uninformed. For example, that mountain over there with the three small peaks lies to the north of your camp; two small streams flow down its sides; Rocky Brook meets Black Brook about a mile south of your camp; the two flow on together to join the Pernaquid River about four miles south from your camp; six miles down, the Pernaquid is the state highway and the railroad. That's the kind of thing you must know— just as Bill and I knew about the wooded road and the brook.

You should always carry a compass, even when you go on fishing trips—there you've got a good laugh on me! And carry matches, too, in a waterproof case. And you should know how to use your compass, which means practice using it. Of course you know that in any regions except the most unsettled parts of the earth, following downstream will lead you almost always to larger streams, which will bring you out to civilization.

All those things are good to know, but none of them is as important as knowing enough not to lose your head and to run wild. Just take it easy, and sit and wait for your friends to come and find you or for daylight or moonlight to help you. Then you'll be okay, and when you get back to camp you'll think it over and decide that it wasn't such a bad experience after all.

Here are some additional valuable insights about finding your way in the woods. They are from *Deep River Jim's Wilderness Trail Book*.

WHICH WAY IS CAMP?

Told by Maurice H. Decker

Do you know the three signs by which woodsmen tell direction when the sun is hidden and they don't have a compass? And what's more important, do you know that only under certain conditions are these three nature signs accurate and reliable? A real woodsman must be able to tell when they can be trusted and when they should be ignored.

At the time I was fifteen, Old Sam Lake, one of Michigan's pioneer hunters, taught me many of the tricks of woodcraft that came as naturally to him as eating and sleeping. This was one of the first skills he taught me. We were out in the timber looking for a deer. Old Sam suddenly dropped the butt of his muzzle-loader on the ground and glanced at me with his keen blue eyes.

"It sure is a good day to get lost," he stated. "Which way is camp?"

I looked at the sky. It was dull and gray. The sun had been hidden for hours. But I remembered how we had turned when we left the cabin door, and I answered glibly enough. "Camp is east of here."

"Which way is east then?"

That had me. Since starting that morning I had tried to keep the different angles of our course straight, but Old Sam had turned and doubled like a rabbit before dogs, and I was completely puzzled. Now I suddenly sensed in his zigzag course and his questions a test of my memory for direction. And I had to stand there silent and mixed up.

"Then yore plumb lost!" Old Sam's tone was scornful. "If I break a leg in some windfall, how you going to get word back for help?"

I had no answer for this disturbing question either.

"If we find out which way is north, can you tell east from that?"

This was a plain insult, but I answered meekly enough, "Facing north, east is on my right."

"Fine," old Sam said. "That's about as much as any tenderfoot knows about the woods. Now we woodsmen use three of Nature's signs to tell north when the sun's hid.

"First is a tree with moss on the bark. Moss grows thickest on the north side, because that is usually shaded

130

and stays damp longer after a rain. See any tree with moss?" I located one, a tall, smooth-barked trunk. Under Sam's guidance I examined the soft growth on all sides with my knife's point. I finally concluded it was thicker on one side.

"You picked a proper tree to test," he admitted grudgingly. "I don't know whether it was an accident or not, but remember which way the thick moss faced. Now come on over to this thicket. I want to show you why you can't always trust the first sign you find. I'm going to show you that even Nature lies at times, like some folks I know."

I followed to the thick stand of timber. Sam pointed. "Every trunk here has moss on. See if the thickest growth is on the side you think faces north."

I jabbed rapidly with my blade and in a few minutes made a disconcerting discovery. The heaviest layer of moss on several trees faced as many directions. Something was wrong here. Moss had no business pointing north and east and west. I turned a perplexed face to the old woodsman.

"Now I reckon you see what I mean. A fellow must average up the woods signs before he can be right. Never believe one and take it for granted. You have to use only natural signs too; these are unnatural."

I waited anxiously for the explanation. "Moss," resumed Old Sam, "grows where there's moisture, which, in natural cases, is on the north side of a tree where the sun don't strike. But you've got to find the right tree. Always hunt a smooth-barked one that stands out alone or at the edge of thicker stands. The trees here grow so close they shade each other and we find heavy moss on three sides in place of but one."

I began to see a new angle to the art of woodcraft. Plainly enough, Nature's signs could be unreliable in certain circumstances.

"Look at that leaning tree," ordered Sam. "It tells you a lie, too. The topside bark has caught more rain and

131

snow than the others and stays damp, making the moss grow heavier. That side of the tree don't point north by a jugful. And here's a tree that broke over in some brush. The moss is heaviest on the bottom, 'cause the brush has held the wet and kept the sun off.

"Neither can you trust the moss sign on a tree that grows in the shadow of a mountain or a big rock. A woodsman wouldn't, but some danged tenderfoot might. He'd jab his knife in, find the thick side and then let out a whoop and rush off in the wrong direction."

Sam paused for breath. This was a long speech for his terse nature. "That tree you picked first is probably telling the truth. The east, south, and west sides have a chance to dry off after a wet spell, and only the north grows heavy moss. Now if you hunted up two or three more like it and they all agreed, you could reasonably think you were on the right trail.

"But there's other signs. A woodsman can't afford not to be thorough, especially when he cruises alone. He looks at the growth rings and bark thickness on big old trees. The rings will be wider and the bark thicker on the north side."

Sam handed me his hatchet, a narrow-bitted tomahawk that had crushed the marrow bones of many deer.

"Cut a shallow notch in that big tree on the side you think is north from the moss sign. Then cut another notch opposite the first one."

I obeyed and carefully examined the bark and growth rings exposed. It took keen eyes, but the difference was there, and I was elated. This sign checked with the first.

"Not so bad," Sam grunted. "Now you got two signs to agree. You've got somewhere. But remember, it's a life and death matter to be lost sometimes, so you better check what we've learned by the third and last sign. It isn't as reliable as these first two, but I use it when I doubt them."

132

Sam looked about him. "The tips of pines, spruce, hemlock, and like trees are supposed to turn toward the rising sun," he stated. "They face the east or a little south of east. I see one ahead—go look."

I ran to the tree but was conscious of fresh disappointment. The slender tip pointed directly opposite from the way I had decided was east. Sam watched my glum face with evident pleasure.

"This one's a freak," I concluded. "We can't trust it, but why, I don't know. It's growing here by itself with no other timber to shade or shield it."

Sam chuckled. "I'll tell you why. That tree grows where it's exposed to storms. The winds come rip-snorting down between the hills on each side and their draft has turned the tip away from its natural way of facing."

"Then," I cried, "we'll find one that stands where seasonal storms don't hit it squarely. That tree won't lie."

In spite of his age, Old Sam rolled along over the rough ground with an ease that taxed my young muscles and wind. Finally he paused, and I looked up at a towering hemlock.

"There's your third sign—pointing so it agrees with the others. So that way is east. We know it for sure now." He led me over a couple of hills—right up to the cabin door.

Of course, Old Sam had known where camp was all along. He had used this cleverly practical stunt to teach me woodcraft signs so I would never forget them, and I never have.

When a woodsman searches for direction signs, he must examine each sign closely to see whether it has been distorted by unusual conditions and unnatural influences. If it has, he discards it. Then he averages up those signs that he trusts and checks one by another. He never relies on a single sign if there are any others against which to check it.

By the way, if you're ever lost in the snow and get thirsty, do not eat snow. Snow not only fails to satisfy, but it also makes one weak.

Here is what you can do when it snows and you need water to drink. When snow is so deep that it covers small brooks or pools to such a depth that no drinking place is afforded, take a stick of sufficient length and thrust it through the snow until an open passage is made to the water. Dip the stick in water, then in the snow, repeating the process until you have formed a water-soaked snowball. From this you can suck the water.

WATERPROOFING MATCHES

You know how important matches are in the woods, and how worthless they are when they become wet. Here's a good way to keep them waterproof. Melt some paraffin in an empty soup can over the stove, and pour it into a box of matches. When it cools you will have your matches encased safely against moisture. You can even drop them into the water without fear that they'll get wet. Just dig one out when you need it. Scratch it against a rock, and away it'll burn.

CRICKETS AS THERMOMETERS

Crickets are the woodsman's thermometer. To get the temperature accurately you need a watch with a second hand. Count the number of chirps that the crickets make in fifteen seconds, then add forty, and there you have it. Let's say that the crickets chirp twenty-one times in fifteen seconds. Twenty-one plus forty makes sixty-one—and that's the Fahrenheit temperature—or close to it. If you check this with a thermometer you'll find that the crickets and the little glass tube agree within one or two degrees.

You've noticed probably that crickets usually chirp in unison, and the warmer it is the faster they chirp. In cold weather the cricket thermometer won't work, for crickets stop chirping when the thermometer drops to around 50°F.

INDIAN METHOD OF MEASURING TALL OBJECTS

Here is a very practical and reliable method of determining the height of objects. It was much used by Indians of times past, and by an occasional "old timer" of the white race, too.

Suppose you want to measure the height of a tree, for example. Walk from the base of the tree to a point from which, on bending over and looking between your legs, you can just see the top of the tree. Mark the spot where you are first able to see the top of the tree. The distance you have paced is the same as the height of the tree.

Of course, you should know the length of your average stride, so that you can figure the distance in feet that you have walked. Then, too, you must figure out for yourself, using some object of which you know the height, just how far you should lean forward when sighting between your legs. After a few trials you can determine exactly how far downward you must lean to get consistent results. In bending over, some Indians place their hands on their knees; others grasp their ankles. Either way may be used.

The factor that makes this Indian method practical is that you always have handy your measuring tools—your head, hands, legs, and feet.

COLLECTING ANIMAL TRACKS

Make a wooden frame four inches square with sides about an inch and a half deep. Varnish this frame, especially in the corners, to prevent leaking. When taking a print, place the frame over the track and press it about one quarter of an inch into the ground. Then make a liquid mixture of plaster of Paris and water, being careful not to add so much water that the mixture won't dry quickly. Too much water will also decrease the strength of your print.

Now pour the liquid into the frame so that the print is well covered, and let it stay until thoroughly dry. Then very carefully remove the cast from the frame, clean it thoroughly, and varnish it all over. You now have what is called the negative cast.

When the varnish is dry, grease the print side and replace the negative in the frame. Then pour another mixture of plaster of Paris over the print side of the negative. When this has hardened, take it from the frame and varnish it. You will then have the track just as it was imprinted in the earth. Greasing the sides of the frame will make it easier to remove the cast.

A NARROW ESCAPE

By Archibald Rutledge, outdoorsman, 1880

One day long ago I found the nest of a black pleated woodpecker in a hole in a large bay tree. This woodpecker is black and white, with a scarlet crest on his head, and is one of the largest members of this family of birds.

I wanted to find out if there were eggs in the nest, so I climbed up to the hole. Just as I was about to thrust in my arm, I heard a faint stir in the hollow. A sound from such a place is always exaggerated. Could one of the birds be at home? I put my hand up to the hole, hesitating, not wishing to disturb the mother, if she happened to be in. I thumped against the trunk of the tree, as such a jar is always likely to bring an inhabitant out of a hole. But no sound came. Then, standing on tiptoe, I began to thrust my hand through the aperture, and downward. In another moment I was drawing it out gingerly, hardly daring to breathe, for an odor had come to me, which, once identified, is never forgotten: a smell of oily cucumbers, if you can imagine such a thing, a not especially unpleasant smell unless you happen to know what kind of creature gives it off.

Jumping to the ground, I got away as fast as possible. But as soon as I had procured an axe from the house, I was back at the scene, making chips fly from the bay tree. As the tree was not large and was partly hollow, it was soon down. Not waiting for me to slit open the tree, the venomous creature that had there taken up his temporary abode began to slide from the hole, sounding his rattles ominously as he came.

A great diamond-back rattler it was, which proved by later measurements to be seven feet five inches long. After I had killed him, I investigated and found in his distended body the mother black pleated woodpecker and her five eggs. Doubtless he had mounted the tree by way of an old stump; then, aided by some greenery leaning against the bay, he had entered the home of these beautiful birds. The other woodpecker was nowhere to be seen.

That was a narrow escape for me. My hand must have been within a few inches of that great spade-shaped head, those eyes of bloodshot topaz, those deadly jaws. But for the warning of that faint but unmistakable odor, I might not have been alive today.

Ever since then it has seemed to me that one of the most foolhardy things a person can do is to put his hand into

137

places into which he cannot see—such as under a rock crevice or over some obstacle on a bank that he is climbing, or in a tree-hollow. In the wilderness, danger lurks in just such places.

TREATING A SNAKE BITE

If possible, apply a tourniquet between the wound and the heart. Suck the wound immediately, spitting out the saliva. There is no danger in being poisoned this way if you have no open sores in your mouth or on your lips. Don't give a person bitten by a snake any alcohol. It will do him more harm than good. Get to a hospital as soon as possible. Remain as calm as possible to keep blood circulation at a minimal. Take comfort in the fact that very few people die from rattlesnake bites in America.

CAMPFIRE CRAFT

A green backlog fire for broiling or frying.

Three or four ½ inch square iron rods laid across logs or stones make an ideal camp grate.

Clean sooty kettles with gritty mud or sand and water.

Two green logs for two or three pots or pans and a handy place to set things

Iron rods across a hole scooped out of a clay bank.

A three log fire as used by Seminole Indians. As the ends burn away, the logs are pushed towards the center.

Two good old methods

A simple pole crane. The end of the pole may be pointed and pushed or driven into the ground.

Make pit 2' wide

Sectional view of bean-hole or corn pit, faced with stones to hold the heat. A sloping front facilitates the removal of ashes.

A three stone fire. See that pan rests evenly before starting fire.

A simple pot-hook.

A thin flat stone supported by stones with a small fire under it makes an excellent warming plate to keep food warm.

FIRES
BY W. BEN. HUNT, HALES CORNERS, WIS.

A two stone fire can be used for more than one kettle or pan.

Don't build fires close to live trees. It may injure or kill them.

Don't build fires against dead trees or logs. It may start a fire that you can't put out.

Don't have dry grass or rubbish near a fire. It may start a grass or forest fire.

Don't leave a fire unattended. Always put it out when you go away.

Don't try to build a fire with green wood. After a rain, remember that high wood is dry wood.

Don't carry loose matches in your pockets. Keep them in a small bottle well corked or in a water-proof match safe. Dry matches are worth more to you in wet weather than in dry weather.

Don't build a large fire for cooking, unless it's to get embers to bake beans or roast corn.

And Remember-soft wood and small branches for a quick fire & hardwood and knots for a hot fire.

A one stone fire. See that pot rests evenly & firmly.

Always hang cooking kettles up off of ground

A safe stove for tepee or wigwam

Do not cut thru rim.

Opening may be closed to hold fire.

Cut sides of vent and bend inwards.

A dandy stove can be made from an old powder can or galvanized pail. Clay banked around the base helps to hold the heat.

If your camp is near a cut bank, a permanent fireplace may be built like this. A piece of sheet iron makes a better top than stone

Make the chimney hole first. You may have to try some other place if you strike a large stone or root.

Place stones around top of chimney.

HELP PREVENT FOREST FIRES

STARTING A FIRE WITH FLINT AND STEEL

Four items are needed to start a fire with flint and steel:

1. Charred cloth to catch the spark (see instructions)
2. Flint or quartz
3. Steel
4. Tinder

To start the fire, do the following: (See Figure 47.)

1. Place tinder on the ground or a solid surface. For tinder use binder twine or string. Unravel about twelve inches of the string, and form it into a sort of bird nest. Other good tinder is shredded bark of cedar, fine wood chips, and very dry tall grass and weeds. The Indians used to store these in late summer and use the grass throughout the winter.

2. Place charred cloth on top of the tinder to catch a spark.

3. Hold flint and steel firmly with your fingers.

4. Strike the edges of the steel and flint against each other using vertical, glancing blows. Shower enough hot sparks into the charred cloth to start the fire.

5. When a spark is caught in the charred cloth and begins to glow, place it in the tinder.

6. Lift tinder bird nest in your hands, and blow briskly on the charred cloth until the flame starts. Do not be afraid of burning your hands, because you're moving quickly.

7. To master this skill, the secret is good charred cloth, very dry tinder, and practice, practice, practice.

Force sparks to fall on cloth.

Store cloth in a tin to protect it and keep it dry. Do not put flint and cloth in the same tin, because the flint would tear the cloth apart.

Hold tinder nest in hands and blow until the flame appears. Do not be afraid of burning your hands since it flames fairly quickly and placing the flamed cloth and straw into the wood pile happens too quickly for you to get burned.

Figure 47

HOW TO MAKE CHARRED CLOTH FOR FLINT AND STEEL

MATERIALS NEEDED:
Cotton cloth—make sure it is pure, and the older the better. An old dish towel or cloth diaper works well.
Scissors
Hot plate
Empty coffee can for heating the cloths

141

Another empty can or tin that is airtight and sealed, for storing the charred cloths (for example, a candy tin with a tight lid). You can purchase clean, empty cans at paint stores.

1. Cut cotton cloth into discs the same diameter as the airtight can.

2. Place seven to ten cloth discs in the coffee can. Place can on a hot plate. *Do the heating outside, since the cloth emits a bad smell and smoke.* (Open fire may be used, like a barbeque or camp fire.)

3. Allow cloth to char until it is black, usually about 15-30 minutes.

4. Place charred discs in airtight can to keep dry for future use. Keep flint in separate container.

TOMAHAWK THROWING

Ever since I (Little Bear) saw an old Hollywood movie depicting an Indian throwing a tomahawk at an enemy, I knew then and there I would have to develop the skill. At the ripe old age of twelve, I began to throw "hawks" at my huge Magnolia tree in Santa Monica, California. Little did I realize then the Lord would use the skill later in my life in many Christian camp settings throughout America, to starry-eyed youth longing for a touch of the past.

Before attempting this skill, secure a reliable tomahawk with a stout handle. (See resource listing at the end of this book for details about purchasing a good hawk.)

Be sure the hawk head is secure on the handle before throwing. The secret is distance and form. A tomahawk must turn one complete revolution in the air before it will stick in the target. For the average-size person with the average-size hawk, six paces is about the right distance for one revolution, twelve paces for twice the distance. However, become skilled at one revolution before trying to throw at a great distance.

After stepping off your paces, grip the hawk firmly by the end of the handle, with the hawk blade vertical with the target. Take one step forward, at the same time throwing the hawk in an overhead swing, much as you would throw a rock or baseball. Keep your swing smooth and your wrist straight. If the hawk does not hit on the blade, adjust your pace until you find the right distance. You may also need to adjust your swing so you throw neither too hard nor too lightly. Always observe basic safety rules when throwing the hawk, and have all spectators *behind* you at all times. With practice, you too can become proficient and accurate with the tomahawk.

CARRYING AND THROWING
THE TOMAHAWK

1. Take five steps from target. At this distance of ten feet, the tomahawk makes two turns and strikes.
2. Hold the butt end of the handle in the middle of the palm of the hand.

3. Keep feet apart with weight of body resting on the right leg.
4. Fix eyes on target— not the tomahawk.
5. Throw tomahawk forward smartly.
6. Do not jerk the handle back when throwing. This would brand you as a namby-pamby with unmistakable lady-like qualities.

A. The private of the 11th Regiment of Virginia carries his tomahawk in a belt loop.
B. The militiaman wears a shoulder belt with a double frog for his tomahawk and bayonet.

Figure 48

KNIFE THROWING

Another skill I developed was knife throwing. It is best to use a knife that is designed for throwing. It is very easy to break the blade of an ordinary thin-blade knife if you use it for throwing. Believe me, I broke plenty. Knives have to be made of spring steel and can be purchased at the Dixie Gun Works. (See resource list at end.)

The secret of knife throwing is also distance and form. However, it is much more difficult to get the right pace and the right form for knife throwing than it is for tomahawk throwing.

The knife may be thrown either by the blade or by the handle. It is thrown in an overhead swing, much as you would throw a rock.

Each individual must establish the proper distance for his knife to do one revolution in the air before hitting the target. This varies with the length of a person's arm and the size of the knife. The individual must also use exactly the same form each time. Since the knife must hit on a very small point, it takes a great deal of precision to be accurate. This skill, therefore, will require much practice.

Knife throwing can be dangerous. Be sure to follow basic safety rules at all times when throwing a knife.

RIFLEMAN'S HOMEMADE
HUNTING KNIFE

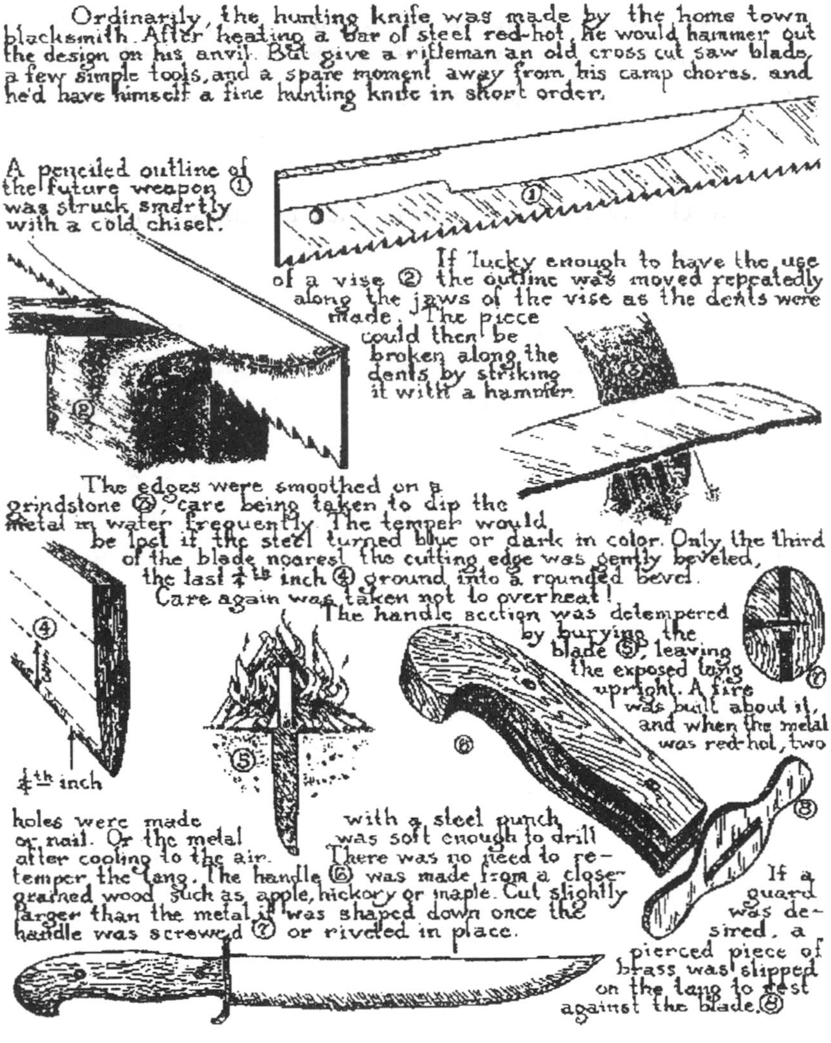

Ordinarily, the hunting knife was made by the home town blacksmith. After heating a bar of steel red-hot, he would hammer out the design on his anvil. But give a rifleman an old cross cut saw blade, a few simple tools, and a spare moment away from his camp chores, and he'd have himself a fine hunting knife in short order.

A penciled outline of the future weapon ① was struck smartly with a cold chisel.

If lucky enough to have the use of a vise ② the outline was moved repeatedly along the jaws of the vise as the dents were made. The piece could then be broken along the dents by striking it with a hammer.

The edges were smoothed on a grindstone ③ care being taken to dip the metal in water frequently. The temper would be lost if the steel turned blue or dark in color. Only the third of the blade nearest the cutting edge was gently beveled, the last ¾th inch ④ ground into a rounded bevel. Care again was taken not to overheat! The handle section was detempered by burying the blade ⑤, leaving the exposed tang upright. A fire was built about it, and when the metal was red-hot, two

¾th inch

holes were made with a steel punch or nail. Or the metal was soft enough to drill after cooling to the air. There was no need to re-temper the tang. The handle ⑥ was made from a close-grained wood such as apple, hickory or maple. Cut slightly larger than the metal it was shaped down once the handle was screwed ⑦ or riveted in place.

If a guard was desired, a pierced piece of brass was slipped on the tang to rest against the blade.⑧

Figure 49

146

HORN CRAFT

Making your own powder horn, salt horn, or blowing horn not only brings a lot of enjoyment, but also provides a great deal of satisfaction. The personal value also increases when it is handmade.

First, select a good basic horn. If you plan to engrave the horn, it should be light or white in the areas you plan to engrave. A horn with a black tip and a white body looks handsome indeed.

If the horn is raw, you need to boil the horn and clean out the membranes from the inside. Boil outside—the smell is obnoxious. File or sand off the rough exterior down to the smooth horn. Sometimes you can buy horns from blackpowder gun shops already cleaned and semi-polished. I picked up my horns from a farm where the cattle are dehorned yearly. Look around your area to see if you can find raw horns; it is an experience you will never forget.

1. Saw off the open end until you have smooth, even edges.

2. Cut off the tip of the horn and bore a small hole into the center cavity. It should be just large enough for the powder to flow freely from the horn, about the size of a matchstick. For the blowing horns I have made, I made my holes the size of a trumpet mouthpiece. I drilled one smaller hole, then a larger one like a mouthpiece. I took sandpaper and formed a nice-feeling blowing tip.

3. For a powder horn or a salt horn, cut and carve a wooden plug for the large end of the horn. The plug should be about the size of the opening with a slight taper on the end. Be careful not to make it too small. The plug should have a ridge or overhang slightly larger than the opening.

4. Boil the horn until it is soft and pliable.

5. Drive the plug into the end of the horn while it is still soft.

6. Once plug is in place, secure the plug with nails or wooden pegs. I used small copper tacks that would age over time, making the horn look older.

7. When the horn cools and hardens, it will conform and seal around the plug.

8. Grind or sand the plug to the desired shape. You can stain the wooden plug to your heart's desire.

9. Carve a small plug or stopper out of hardwood for the small end of the horn. Make the small end long enough to fit well into the horn. For variety and uniqueness, carve the stopper into the shape of an acorn, animal's head, bird's head, or other shape.

10. Some horn makers will carve or grind grooves, ridges, or other shapes on the small end of the horn. You will need at least one groove for your carrying strap.

11. Instead of sanding, some horn makers prefer to scrape down their horns with the edge of a piece of glass. This gives the horn a semifinish without polishing.

12. You may wish to scrape down your horn so it is thin enough to see how much powder you have when held up to a light. If so, this should be done before engraving the horn.

13. If you wish to engrave your horn, this is referred to as *scrimshaw*, which is done in the following steps.

SCRIMSHAW PROCEDURE

A. Draw the design on your horn with a felt-tip pen. Old-timers drew such things as animals, birds, Indian designs, ships, hunting scenes, or whatever suited their fancy. Use your imagination.

B. Spray with hair spray or fixer to prevent smearing.

C. With the point of a knife or other sharp instrument, etch or scratch the design well into the horn.

D. Cover the design with black ink or thin paint.

E. Before the ink or paint has a chance to dry, wipe off all the excess, leaving only the residue in the scratch marks. This will bring out your design in bold, dark lines.

F. You may seal the design further with a coat of wax.

G. Polish the horn to the desired finish. I used car wax.

H. Secure a leather shoulder strap for carrying the horn.

NOTE: A salt horn is made in much the same way as a powder horn, except the salt horn is much smaller.

POWDER HORN

Oxen and cattle horns were trimmed on both ends, then a hole bored into the tip to connect with the horn cavity. After carefully scraping down to proper thickness with the knife, and cutting in the distinctive design, a pine plug was whittled to fit the wide end. This was tacked permanently in place with small nails. The horn was filled with powder through the drilled hole.

The American militia and riflemen could ask for no handier a powder container. Easy to come by, light to carry, ready-shaped for pouring, and fire and water-resistant, the powder horn found favor with other branches of the army. Outsized supply or "Mother" horns were used to fill more conventional horns and were carried by the cannon crews to prime their pieces. Frequently, officers loaded their pistols from small, easily carried horns. Even the infantry were issued regular horns when the supply of cartridge boxes were exhausted.

When camp duties permitted, the horn was scraped thin and smooth so that the amount of powder could be seen when held to the light. Then all manner of designs were cut or engraved into the surface. Even these carvings were practical for they served as road maps to the American countryside. In addition, engravings of the enemy uniforms helped identify those hostile to the cause of liberty.

Oxen, of course, had right and left horns. A right-handed soldier used a right-sided horn, for it snugged his hip well, the tip pointed forward for loading and upward to prevent spillage. Therefore, a right or left-handed soldier could be identified by the powder horn he carried.

JOHN BALL His Horn
Dec'r 19, 1776

Figure 50

150

Back in 1979, I was as poor as dirt, but rich in creative ideas. I wanted to secure a historical period hunting outfit like the ones the old pioneers may have had. With no money to buy such an outfit, I decided to make my own. Surprisingly, it turned out better than I had expected. To get material I shopped the thrift stores and bought just the right material from various coats. I altered it to fit at half the cost of new fabric. Below is a pattern for you to make your own hunting shirt.

MAKING A HUNTING SHIRT

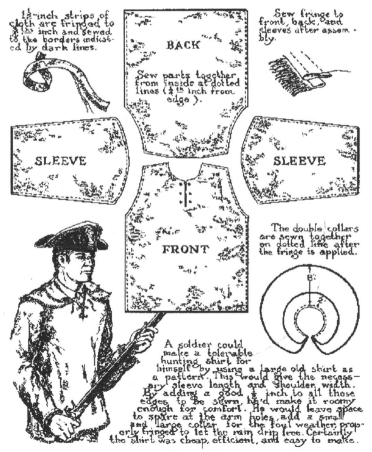

1½-inch strips of cloth are fringed to ½ inch and sewed to the borders indicated by dark lines.

BACK

Sew parts together from inside at dotted lines (¼ th inch from edge).

Sew fringe to front, back, and sleeves after assembly.

SLEEVE

SLEEVE

FRONT

The double collars are sewn together on dotted line after the fringe is applied.

A soldier could make a tolerable hunting shirt for himself by using a large old shirt as a pattern. This would give the necessary sleeve length and shoulder width. By adding a good ½ inch to all those edges to be sewn he'd make it roomy enough for comfort. He would leave space to spare at the arm holes, add a small and large collar for the foul weather, properly fringed to let the rain drip free. Certainly the shirt was cheap, efficient, and easy to make.

Figure 51
151

When I have worn my frontier outfit around the country, many young people have asked me what the funny looking wooden thing is next to my bag. Well, here it is for you to make for your own outfit.

THE NATURAL TREE NOGGIN

RIFLEMAN'S NOGGIN ~ Trees healed old scars by means of a gnarled growth, and from these burls a rifleman could carve himself a handy noggin. The better burls were found on apple, cherry, maple, birch and oak trees. This section was sawed off close to the tree trunk, with a projection left on one side for the handle. With the wood "green" and more easily carved, the inside was whittled out - a curved chisel made this easier - after pilot holes were drilled.

Because the bark protected the outer surface, it was not removed until the inside of the cup was finished. To prevent checking and cracking, the modern-day whittler might soak the noggin overnight in linseed oil.

The handle was carved and drilled for a leather thong, and on the other end a wooden toggle was knotted in place. This was shoved under the rifleman's belt, and held there by pressure, ready for the first cool drink of spring water.

WOODEN DRINKING MUG - A circular series of holes was drilled into a block of hard wood. A mug-sized cylindrical hole was then carved out. The outside was roughly shaped with a chisel or tomahawk, then whittled smooth.

Figure 52

152

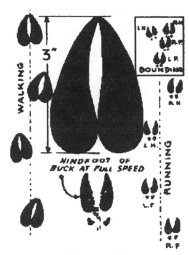

Figure 53

THE SECRET OF SILENT STALKING

When I am out hunting and have a young future hunter with me, or an unskilled old-timer, would-be hunter, I am always amazed at how much noise he makes while walking. Follow these simple rules, and you will be far ahead of the average unlearned city slicker.

Pay close attention to your feet. Try to avoid committing your weight to each step before you know that it will make little or no noise. The Indian gait is described often as "pigeon-toed," but that description is inaccurate. Most Indians pointed their toes straight ahead and walked tirelessly on the balls of their feet. Most white men put the weight on the heel; then the ball slaps down. If you listen to most men walking on a hard surface, you'll discover that each step produces two noises, one made by the heel, and one made by the ball of the foot.

There is no way to lessen the weight if an obstacle is encountered, because the man strides along heavily and carelessly. If the heel doesn't snap a twig, the forward part of the foot will. Most white men also turn their toes outward to some extent so that the inner side of the foot is likely to catch obstacles. The Indian's walk is ideal for getting through thick growth quietly.

It is not necessary, however, to walk exactly like an early American Indian. If you try to point the feet straight forward when you are unaccustomed to it, the calves of your legs and ankles will soon give out under the strain. Yet, if you do pay attention to how you walk and try to do so quietly, you'll soon be walking more like an Indian or moccasin-wearing frontiersman with every mile covered. Try to feel with your toes so that you can withdraw your foot if you feel a noise-making obstruction underneath it. Without this ability, you'll have to look down much of the time to pick out suitable ground, and that will keep your eyes off the game. Some hunters are so agile that they can look ahead and hardly ever look down. It almost seems as if their feet have eyes.

For years I have practiced walking with one foot in front of the other, single file. This creates a natural line which takes less room on the ground in the field. Since I have traveled for over twenty years throughout airports, I have enjoyed watching people walk. It is truly amazing how few walk in a straight pace. If you practice this walk, it will become a natural, effortless habit.

TRACKING

I have always been fascinated by the art of tracking. Several years ago I read a book by a man named Tom Brown, called *The Tracker*. The book tells of how as a boy, Tom learned to track from an old Indian who had learned the skill from his father. If you are interested in this book, search the web and purchase an old copy.

I must admit I can write only about others' experiences and not my own in this field. First, certain hunting areas are not conducive to tracking game for miles in hope of a shot with a camera or rifle. In South Texas where I have the privilege to hunt on a private ranch, the terrain is so hostile and bushy that to track is impossible. In Oregon where I used to hunt, the terrain was so dense that without the skill of an Indian you could not even see tracks. However, if you happen to live in those ideal areas where there are open spaces and perhaps snowfalls during the hunting season, by following these skills you may get the thrill of tracking and bagging wild meat for the table.

TELLING A DOE TRACK
FROM A BUCK TRACK

There is really no sure way to tell the difference between the tracks of a big doe and a buck, but there are a few guidelines that sometimes work. Big prints moving alone are often those of a mature buck. Yearling deer follow their dams, and one doe may even have a pair of twins following her. Since does and antlerless fawns are usually protected by law, it is usually unwise to follow the tracks of a group of deer. Bucks usually move alone, but during the rut (their mating season in late fall), they run with does. If you find tracks of does and fawns and then a big track joins them, there's a chance that you will soon come upon a buck.

Bucks seem to drag their feet a little more than does, and they therefore often make scrapes or drag marks behind each print in soft ground or snow when they are walking slowly. However, this is not always the case.

To tell a fresh track from an old track also takes years of practice. On damp ground shaded by trees or brush, a week-old track may look very fresh. The disturbed pine needles or leaves may still be damp on their undersides, and the little clods of earth thrown up by a running deer may still be dark with moisture. Follow such a track long enough, and you'll probably come to a dry place. If the tracks there are still fresh, you are probably close to a deer. Only good tracking snow makes the story clear, but snow seldom seems to fall during the short deer-hunting season. Good tracking snow is slightly damp and takes prints well, and it falls the preceding night. If snow falls before you go hunting, every track is fresh. If snow is still falling when you begin to hunt, it may fill up the prints before you get close to the deer.

HOW INDIANS TRACKED AND ELUDED THEIR ENEMIES

Early in life Indian boys were taught to observe the tracks of birds and animals and to recognize their calls. They were taught that each bird and animal had a seasonal call or cry, and that it differed in spring and autumn. They were shown the moccasins of different tribes and told how to recognize the footmarks of these moccasins. They were even instructed in the minute differences in clothing, painting, smells, food, customs, and habits of the various tribes around them, and how to recognize a tribe by a snatch of conversation.

The older men in taking a company of boys on a hike would make a contest in observing things, and they often awarded a small prize to the most proficient. Then they would sit around a campfire and tell how they had tracked their foes or had eluded them. Boys soon understood that it was quite necessary to know the "secret language of the trail," a language written in signs and sounds that the ordinary eye and ear know nothing about. When white men and boys were captured and adopted, they were instructed how to know the woods and what was in them. Some have written of their experiences so we have a way of knowing how true it was that the Indians knew the ways of the forest.

In John Heckewelder's interesting old account of the Pennsylvania Indians, he mentions the Indian raid upon

156

the settlers on the Big Mahanoy, where fourteen whites were killed.

The survivors were shocked and enraged. They determined that if the Indians had fallen upon them they would kill the first Indian they could find. It so happened that Luke Holland, an affable Indian of the Lenape tribe, was among them, and had long been known as a friendly and inoffensive fellow. Even his name was one that the whites had given him, in respect for his friendliness. The esteem of the whites was turned to hatred, however, when they beheld their friends and relatives dead, and knew that others had been carried off into captivity. Poor Indian Luke tried to explain that his people were peaceful and that the deed must have been committed by a party of Mingoes. The whites would not listen but determined to have their revenge. In desperation Luke begged that if a party of men would go with him he would surely find the raiders and prove that they were not of his nation.

The whites at length consented, but they threatened his life if he showed the least treachery. Luke led them to a secluded spot on a rocky part of the mountain, tracking the unseen enemy over ground where the whites could see no marks whatsoever. This excited great suspicion, and they thought that the Indian had led them away from the trail so the enemy would be able to escape.

With great pains Luke showed his party that there were bits of moss that had been loosened, sticks that had been moved, small pebbles that had been rolled aside, moss on the rocks that had been pressed with the human foot, and other evidences that a number of men had passed by. He could see all these things as he hurried along, but the white men with him had to stoop over and look at the ground to see what he pointed out. Finally Luke told them that he would soon show them the footprints of the enemy. Shortly they came out on softer ground, and there, sure enough, were the prints of moccasined feet. The Indian explained that there were eight men in the enemy's party and that the camp was not far off. The pursuers crossed the valley and climbed a neighboring height from which they plainly saw the enemy making their evening camp. Some were asleep and others were drawing off their leggings. Swinging on the scalp poles were the scalps they had taken.

"See, there is the enemy!" whispered the Lenape. "They are not of my nation, but Mingoes, as I truly told you. They are in our power. Come on, we are nearly two to one. Come on and you will have your revenge!"

The settlers, as Heckewelder says, were overcome with fear and would not take up the fight. They urged Luke to lead them home by the nearest route, which he did, whereupon they told a lively story about discovering the enemy in numbers so great that they did not dare attack.

Not all settlers were afraid, however, and some learned to track as ably as the most subtle native. It is the art of tracking that makes a real woodsman and frontiersman. There is nothing mysterious about it, for it is all a matter of practiced observation.

When the enemy pursues, safety demands a quick and skillful retreat. This is sometimes difficult when the enemy is also quick and skillful, but old warriors have told me how they escaped when death seemed upon their heads.

Of course much of the success in escaping depended upon how many pursuers there were. If they spread out in a long thin line the difficulty was increased. If there were only one man chasing a victim, there was a much better chance of getting away.

Many of the old legends tell of boys who escaped monsters by crawling into hollow logs, feet first, of course, and then piling up rotten wood before their faces. In one tale a youth found a good log and crawled in just as a spider let itself down and spun a web over the opening. The pursuers suspected the log but were deceived by the web. With many tribes the spider is a sacred creature and never killed, but whether the belief springs from such a legend or not is not easy to tell.

In the woods it was sometimes easy to get out of sight quickly by climbing into the branches of a thick-leaved tree, or into a pine or hemlock. By clinging to the trunk and keeping very quiet, the one being chased had a good chance, but if once discovered, he was a shining mark for arrows.

An old Indian with a white name of Dondey once told me that he escaped pursuit by crawling into a hollow tree but found it an uncomfortable place. He also told a story of how a man in such a place was discovered because he looked through a knothole.

There are tales of youths who escaped by quickly diving and then swimming under water to a convenient spot along the bank where they could put their heads up under the protruding bank.

There are stories of maidens and boys without weapons who were chased through the tall grass of the plains, and yet who escaped when the foe seemed directly upon them. They crawled into the carcass of a frozen buffalo that had been eaten out by wolves. It must have been an unsavory refuge, but it was better than torture.

Two old scouts once told me how they had escaped by burrowing under the leaves of the forest mold and piling branches over themselves. One described how he had disappeared in the desert by having a blanket smeared with pitch and covered with sand. He simply dug a little hollow the size of his body and then lay down in it and covered himself with his blanket. When his pursuer came in sight there was nothing to see but sand everywhere.

In all these tricks, the utmost care had to be taken not to leave tell-tale tracks. Tracks or other signs were sure to be seen right around the hiding place, and caution had to be displayed in attracting the enemy from the scent. This was often done by false leads, as by running in the soft soil of a riverbank, as if one had jumped in, and then back-tracking to harder ground.

Back-tracking is a real art, because a skilled woodsman can tell whether the tracks show walking backward or not. In snow this is especially true. Care must be taken not to drag the foot so as to give away the whole deception.

There were some Indians who were trained as spies and who could disappear right under the noses of their pursuers. Some of these spies carried "false feet" with them, such as the feet of bears, to make tracks in the mud. In this way, they led their pursuers to believe only animals had gone over the trail. The Catawba Indians were reputed to be clever at this type of deception and were greatly feared.

The best plan for getting away when hunted down by the enemy was to create a false trail and then run quietly to a refuge, taking care to cover up any marks, broken twigs, or trampled grass. Where there was danger of being seen, one had to run in such a way that a large rock or tree was kept between the pursuer and the pursued. When the enemy did come into sight, it paid to keep very still. Indians crouched down so as to look like the rocks or clumps of tangled underbrush. An object that is not moving is not easily seen, but once it moves, it immediately attracts the eye.

Most of the forest Indians were cautious about covering up their trails. It took time, but it meant safety. When walking through tall grass they slid their feet through it rather than trampling it by stepping, but if a bunch became bent over they straightened it and moved on. In this manner, when they heard the enemy they kept quiet and, as their tracks were covered, it was not easy to trace them.

When Indians were pursued, they would lie low, keep out of the line of vision, make no noise, cover up their tracks, make a false trail to a jumping-off place, back-track to safety, and if possible lead the pursuer into an ambush where the pursuer would become the victim and not they themselves. It took a real woodsman, an experienced scout, or a clever native to know exactly what to do in all cases.

HOW TO TIE KNOTS

Every boy is familiar with rope and its uses, but not every one is able to handle it to the best advantage. In camping and fishing, and particularly in any sport that has to do with the water, a knowledge of how to tie knots is of the greatest value and interest. Often one's very life depends on a knot holding.

A good knot has three qualities: it must be easy and quick to tie, it must hold fast when pulled tight, and it must be easy to untie. There are a number of knots which meet these requirements but are adapted to different uses.

To learn the various knots which follow, take a section of flexible rope about four feet long and three-eighths of an inch in diameter. To keep the ends from fraying, "whip" or bind them with twine. To do this, make a loop in the twine and lay it on the rope end so that the closed end of the loop projects just over the end of the rope. Begin wrapping with the long end of the twine at a point about an inch from the end of the rope, over the loop and toward the end. When you reach the end of the rope pass the free end of the twine through the loop and pull the other end of the twine. This will pull the free end under the wrapping and secure it. Cut off both ends close to the wrapping.

To understand the directions, learn the following terms:

1. *The Standing-Part* is the long unused portion of the rope upon which the work is done.

2. *The Bight* is the loop formed whenever the rope is turned back upon itself.

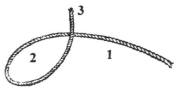

Figure 54
The parts of a knot

3. *The End* is the part used in tying the knots.

162

The two primary knots are the "overhand" and the "figure-of-eight," which must be learned first as a basis for all other knots.

THE OVERHAND KNOT

Beginning with the position shown in the preceding diagram, back the end around the standing-part and up through the bight, drawing it tight.

THE FIGURE-OF-EIGHT KNOT

Make a bight as before. Then lead the end around back of the standing-part and down through the bight. The following knots are chiefly based upon these and can be easily learned by careful study of the diagrams. With practice considerable speed can be obtained, but it is best to "make haste slowly."

THE SQUARE OR REEF KNOT

This is the most common knot for tying two ropes together. It will not slip or jam if properly tied and is easy to untie.

THE FALSE REEF KNOT OR GRANNY

If the ends are not properly crossed in making the reef knot, the granny results, which is a bad and insecure knot.

THE SHEET BEND OR WEAVER'S KNOT

This knot is often used by sailors in bending (tying) the sheet to the clew of the sail and in tying two rope ends together. Make a bight with one rope A, B, then pass the end C, of the other rope up through and around the entire height and bend it under its own standing-part.

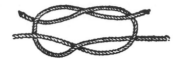

THE BOWLINE

This is one of the most useful of all knots. It forms a loop that will neither jam nor slip and is the only knot which will not cut itself under heavy tension. It is much used on shipboard and in rigging when a loop is desired. To tie the knot, form a small loop on the standing-part, leaving the end long enough for the size of the loop required. Pass the end up through the bight around the standing-part and down through the bight again. To tighten, hold the loop in position and pull the standing-part. It is important that the knot is held firmly in one position while tying, because it is likely to slip before it is tightened. To join two sections together by this knot, tie a bowline in one end, and with the other end form the small

164

loop, then pass the end through the loop of the first bowline to complete the knot. This method should always be used in joining kite cord to prevent cutting.

THE HALTER, SLIP, OR RUNNING KNOT

First form a bight, and then tie an overhand knot around the standing-part. An improvement in this knot for a halter knot is made by forming the overhand knot with a loop in the end which is pulled through. By pulling the end the knot is readily released.

THE SHEEPSHANK

This knot is used to shorten a rope. Take up the amount of rope to be shortened and make a half hitch around each bend as shown. If the knot is to be permanent the ends above each half hitch should be lashed.

THE CLOVE HITCH

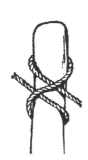

This is a useful knot for quick tying and easy release. It is used in making fast the bow line of a boat in coming into a wharf, in lashing poles together, etc. Hold the standing-part in the left hand and pass the rope around the pole or stake; cross the standing-part, making a second turn around the pole, and pass the end under the last turn. In making a boat secure, form a bight with the end beneath, and throw this over the top of the pile or mooring stake. Form another bight with the end on top, turn this over and throw over pile, pulling end together. This is a very secure knot which can be tied with the greatest speed.

THE FISHERMAN'S BEND

This is a useful knot for use on board a yacht or other boat. Take two turns around a spar or ring, then a half hitch around the standing-part and through the turns on the rings, and another half hitch above it around the standing-part.

THE TIMBER HITCH

This knot is much used in logging operations for hauling logs. Pass the end of the rope around the timber. Then lead it around its standing-part and bring it back to make several turns on its own part. The strain will make it hold securely.

THE DOUBLE HALF HITCH

This is a knot which is easy to tie and will not slip. A neat job may be done by lashing the end to the standing-part after the knot is drawn tight.

THE BECKET HITCH

This knot is useful in fishing to bend a cord or line to a heavier cord or rope. The method is shown.

THE FISHERMAN'S KNOT

This knot is easy to tie and can be readily untied by pulling the two short ends. The ropes are laid alongside each other, and with each end an overhand knot is made around the standing-part of the other. Pull the standing-parts to tighten.

CARRICK BEND

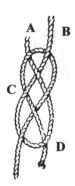

This is a knot which is used principally in joining hawsers for towing or heavy-duty hoisting. Turn the end of one rope A over its standing-part B to form a loop. Pass the end of the other rope across the bight thus formed back of the standing-part B, over the end A, then under the bight at C, passing it over its own standing-part and under the bight again at D.

BLACKWALL HITCH

This knot is used to secure a rope to a hook. The standing-part when hauled tight holds the end firmly.

All About
Shelters
and
Cabins

SHELTERS AND CABINS

I don't know what it is about an outdoor lodge that draws boys. Ever since I can remember, I wanted to live in a log cabin or in a tepee. I must have been influenced by watching Davy Crockett and the Lone Ranger. Being raised in Los Angeles, California, complicated matters because I could not cut down neighborhood trees to make my shelters, so I grew up a bit frustrated. For you who are more fortunate with a backyard or some property, this next section will give you an opportunity to make your own pioneer dwelling to suit your needs.

A WIGWAM

For a wigwam for boys who like to "play Injun" in the backyard, here are some ideas for tepees and wigwams that may easily be carried out at a small cost for the poles and canvas.

Canvas can be bought from some sporting goods or awning companies found in the yellow pages in most phone directories. Poles may be cut in the woods; or one-and-a-half-inch-square fence railing sticks may be purchased at a home repair store and made round with a draw-knife and plane. At the back of this book is listed the address where real tepee polls can be purchased. When cutting poles for a wigwam, select very straight ones, preferably of pine, because crooked or knotty poles are unsightly and make an uneven exterior.

Real Indian tepees are made from buckskin or other strong hides lashed together with rawhide thongs; but as this covering is beyond the reach of the average boy, the next best thing to use will be heavy twilled canvas or stout unbleached muslin. The regulation wigwam is perhaps the most satisfactory kind of tent, because it is roomy, will shed

171

water, and is about the only tent in which a fire may be built without smoking out the occupants. The tepee will not blow over if properly set up and stayed with an anchor-rope, and it is easily taken down and moved from place to place.

For a party of three or four boys, the wigwam shown in Figure 55 will afford ample room, and it is not so large as to be impractical. Select thirteen straight poles, not more than two inches thick at the bottom, and clear them from knots and projecting twigs. They should be ten feet long and pointed at the bottom so as to stick into the ground for a few inches. Tie three of them together eighteen inches from the top, and form a tripod on a circle five feet six inches in diameter. Place the other poles against this tripod to form a cone, as shown in Figure 56, and lash them securely at the top with a piece of clothesline.

From lightweight unbleached muslin or sailcloth, make a cover as shown in Figure 57. Lay out a sixteen-foot circle on a barn floor, a two-car garage, or the grass, with chalk, and indicate an eighteen-inch circle at the middle. Around the outer circle or periphery measure off nineteen feet and chalk-mark the space. From these marks to the center of the circle draw straight lines, and within these limits the area of the wigwam cover will be shown. It should correspond with the plan drawing in Figure 57.

The muslin should be three feet wide. This area can be covered in any direction, sewing the strips together to make the large sheet; or the muslin may be cut in strips three feet wide at one end and tapering to a few inches at the other, as shown in Figure 58, the seams running up and down the canvas instead of across it. The outer edge of the canvas cover should be bound with clothesline or cotton rope, sewed securely with waxed white string. Then thirteen short ropes should be passed over this rope so that the canvas may be lashed securely to the foot of each pole to hold the cover in place.

The doorway flaps are formed by stopping the lacings three feet up from the ground. With short ropes and rings sewed to the cover the flaps may be tied back, as shown in Figure 55.

Real Indian wigwams are decorated with all sorts of emblems, crests, and totems, to identify tribes and families. Boys who make their own tepees can easily invent some mark which will distinguish their tent abode from all others.

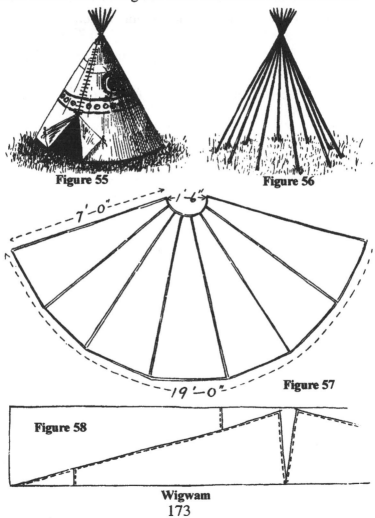

Figure 55

Figure 56

Figure 57

Figure 58

Wigwam
173

Your emblems can even make a statement of your faith and beliefs. Allow the painted ornamentation to dry before stretching the canvas covering over the poles.

A SQUARE TEPEE

A square tepee, as shown in Figure 59, is another form of backyard tent that is easily made. It is not very authentic, but it is creative. Select twelve poles, lash four of them securely, and spread apart on a square of six feet. Add two of the poles to each side, and lash all of them together at the head. Cut four pieces of canvas or heavy unbleached muslin, and make according to the pattern shown in Figure 60. Cut the strips from goods one yard wide. These pieces are six feet long, one foot wide at the head, and six feet at the foot.

Leave the seam open for three feet through the middle of one piece to form the doorway flaps. Sew the four sides together securely with waxed white string. Slip the cover around the pole frame, tie it at the front, and tie it down with short ropes at the foot of each pole. Decorate the cover with paint to give it an Indian appearance. Tie the flaps back to make it easy to go into and out of the tepee.

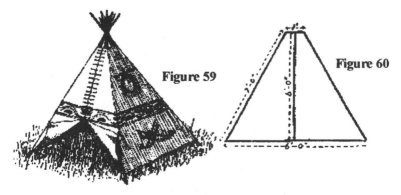

Figure 59

Figure 60

Square Tepee

174

A RIDGE-POLE TEPEE

A ridge-pole tepee, shown in Figure 61, is a simple one to make. It is of one piece of canvas with two flaps sewn at each side to form the ends.

One ridge and two upright poles make the framework, and they are held in place by the canvas, which is drawn and lashed securely to stakes driven in the ground, as may be seen in the drawing. The ridge-pole is eight feet long, one and a half inches thick, and four inches wide. The upright poles are also eight feet long.

Drive metal pegs into the ends of each upright pole. Two inches from either end of the ridge-pole, bore a small hole to insert the pegs, connecting the framework. (See Figure 62, A and B.) Set the upright poles one foot into the ground for good support. Sew widths of muslin together to make the covering, seventeen feet long by eight feet wide. Stretch it over the ridge-pole and fasten down at both sides.

For the back, make a triangular piece of canvas the right size to fit the opening, or cut two flaps, divide at the middle, and tie back, or lace, to close the tent. To make the apron enclosure at the front, cut two pieces of canvas two feet wide, and sew them together along the edges. Attach them together at the middle over the opening.

Cut ten stakes eighteen inches long and two inches wide from hardwood as shown in Figure 62, C. Drive them into the ground at an angle, and attach ropes to the lower edges of the canvas sidings to lash securely to the pegs. This tepee is long enough to swing a hammock from pole to pole, and on a warm summer night it makes an ideal place for sleeping outdoors. The covering also may be decorated with Indian emblems. If a party of boys is going to camp in the backyard, the tepees can be inscribed with different crests and totems to indicate individual ownership.

Figure 61
Ridge-Pole Tepee

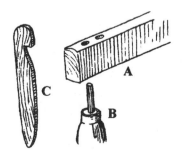

Figure 62
Detail of parts of the
ridge-pole tepee

176

WHERE TO FIND MOUNTAIN GOOSE
AND HOW TO PLUCK AND USE
ITS FEATHERS

Remember that you must use materials at hand in building your shacks, shelters, sheds, and shanties. You are very fortunate if your camp is located in an area where the mountain goose is to be found.

THE MOUNTAIN GOOSE

From Labrador down to the northwestern borders of New England and New York and from there to southwestern Virginia, North Carolina, and Tennessee, the woodsman and camper may make their beds from the feathers of the "mountain goose." The mountain goose is also found inhabiting the frozen soil of Alaska and following the Pacific and the Rocky Mountains the *Abies* make their dwelling-place as far south as Guatemala. Consequently, the *Abies*, or mountain goose, should be a familiar friend of all the scouts who live in the mountainous country, north, south, east, and west.

CHO-KHO-TUNG, SAPIN

I forgot to say that the mountain goose (Figure 63, #1 and #2) is not a bird but a tree. It is humorously called a goose by the woodsmen because they all make their beds of its "feathers." It is the *sapin* of the French-Canadians, the *cho-kho-tung* of the New York Indians, the balsam of the tenderfoot, the Christmas-tree of the little folk, and that particular conifer known by the botanist as *Abies*. There is nothing in nature which has a wilder, more sylvan and charming perfume than the balsam, and the scout who has not slept in the woods on a balsam bed has a pleasure in store for him.

BALSAM

The leaves of the balsam are blunt or rounded at the ends, and some of them are even dented or notched. Each spine or leaf is a scant one inch in length and very flat; the upper part is grooved and of a dark bluish-green color. The underside is much lighter, often almost silvery white. The balsam blossoms in April or May, and the fruit, or cones, stand upright on the branches. These vary from two to four inches in length.

Balsam trees are seldom large, not many of them being over sixty feet high, with trunks from one to less than three feet in diameter. The bark on the trunks is gray in color and marked with horizontal rows of blisters. Each of these blisters contains a small, sticky sap similar to glycerine. Figure 63, #1 shows the cone and leaves of one of the Southern balsams known as the she-balsam, and #2 shows the celebrated balsam-fir tree of the north country, cone and branch.

BALSAM BEDS

The balsam bed is made of the small twigs of balsam trees. Gather twigs of different lengths, from eighteen inches long for the foundation of the bed to ten or twelve inches long for the top layer. If you want to rest well, do not economize on the amount of twigs you gather; many a time a woodsman has had aching bones as a result of being too tired to make his bed properly and attempting to sleep on a thin layer of boughs.

If you attempt to chop off the boughs of balsam, they will resent your effort by springing back and slapping you in the face. You can cut them with your knife, but it is slow work, and you will blister your hands. Take twig by twig with the thumb and fingers (the thumb on top, pointing toward the tip of the bough, and the two forefingers underneath); press down with the thumb, and with a twist of the wrist you can snap the twigs like pipe-stems. Number 3 shows two views of the hands in a proper position to snap off twigs easily and clean. The one at the left shows the hand as it would appear looking down upon it; the one at the right shows the view as you look at it from the side.

PACKING BOUGHS

After collecting a handful of boughs, string them on a stick which you have prepared (see #4). This stick should be of strong, green hardwood, four or five feet long with a fork about six inches long at the butt end to keep the boughs from sliding off. Sharpen it at the upper end so it can be easily poked through a handful of boughs.

String the boughs on this stick as you would string fish, but do it one handful at a time, allowing the butts to point in different directions. It is astonishing to see the amount of boughs you can carry when they are strung on a stick in this manner and thrown over your shoulder as in #5. If you have a lash rope, place the boughs on a loop of the rope, as in #6; then bring the two ends of the rope up through the loop and sling the bundle on your back.

CLEAN YOUR HANDS

When you have finished gathering the material for your bed, your hands will be covered with a sticky sap. A little lard or bacon grease will soften the pitchy substance so it may be washed off with soap and water.

HOW TO MAKE BEDS

To make your bed, spread a layer of the larger boughs on the ground; begin at the head and layer them down to the foot so that the tips point toward the head of the bed, overlapping the butts, as in #7. Continue this until your mattress is thick enough to make a soft couch upon which you can sleep as comfortably as you do at home. Cover the couch with a blanket, and use the bag containing your coat, extra clothes, and sweater for a pillow. Then if you do not sleep well, you must blame the cook.

OTHER BEDDING

If you should happen to be camping in a country destitute of balsam, hemlock, or pine, you can make a good spring mattress by collecting small green branches of any sort of tree which is springy and elastic. Build the mattress as already described. On top of this put a thick layer of hay, straw, or dry leaves or even green material, provided you have a rubber blanket or poncho to cover the latter. In Kentucky an outdoorsman made a mattress of this description and covered the branches with a thick layer of purple ironweed blossoms; over this he spread a rubber army blanket to keep out the moisture from the green stuff. On top of this, he made his bed with his other blankets. It was as comfortable a couch as he had ever slept on; in fact, it was literally a bed of flowers.

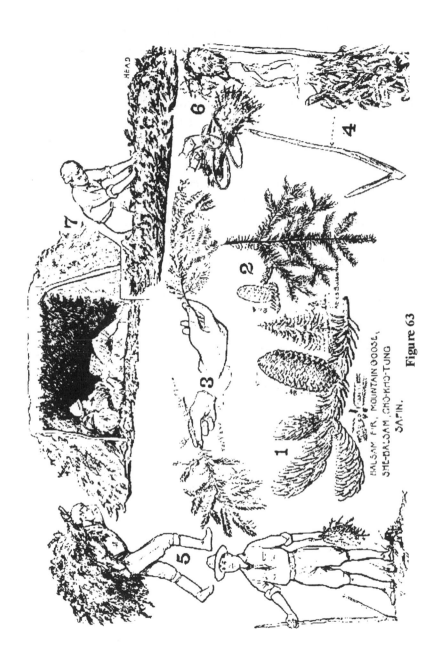

BALSAM FIR, MOUNTAIN GOOSE, SHE-BALSAM, CHO-KHO-TUNG SAPIN.

Figure 63

181

THE HALF-CAVE SHELTER

The first object of a roof of any kind is protection against the weather; no shelter is necessary in fair weather unless the sun in the day or the dampness or coolness of the night causes discomfort. In parts of the West there is so little rain that a tent is often an unnecessary burden, but in the East and the other parts of the country some sort of shelter is necessary for health and comfort.

The original American was always quick to see the advantages offered by an overhanging cliff for a campsite (Figures 64, #9, #10). His simple camps all through the Southwest had gradually turned into carefully built houses long before white men came here. The overhanging cliffs protected the buildings from the rain and weather, and the site was easily defended from enemies. But while these cliff-dwellings had reached the dignity of castles in the Southwest, in the Eastern States—Pennsylvania, for instance—the Iroquois Indians were making primitive camps and using every available overhanging cliff for that purpose.

Today anyone may use a pointed stick on the floor of one of these half caves and unearth, as I have done, numerous potsherds, mussel shells, bone awls, flint arrowheads, split bones of large game animals, and the burnt wood of centuries of campfires which tell the tale of the first lean-to shelter used in America.

HALF CAVES

Half caves are formed when rain and ice cause the lower layers of sandstone cliffs to fall apart. The breaking is often aided by the fine roots of the black birch, rock oak, and other trees and plants. Thus, nature works as a quarryman to produce half caves large enough to shelter a stooping man (see Figure 64, #8, #9, and #10) .

It is sometimes best to make a shelter for the open face of such a cave, even if needed only for a temporary camp (see #10); this may be done by resting poles at a slant against the face of the cliff and over these making a covering of balsam, pine, hemlock, palmetto, palm branches, or any available material for thatch to shed the rain and prevent it from driving under the cliff and soaking our bedding.

WALLS

It is not always necessary to thatch the wall; a number of green boughs with leaves adhering may be rested against the cliffs. Set the boughs upside down so they will shed the rain and not hold it so as to drip into camp. Use your common sense, which will teach you that all the boughs should point downward and not upward as most of them naturally grow. Some men who have taught boys how to make camps have been seen placing the boughs for the lads around the shelter with their branches pointing upward in such a manner that they could not shed the rain. These instructors were city men and apparently thought that the boughs were for no other purpose than to give privacy to the occupants of the shelter, forgetting that the wilderness itself furnishes privacy.

The half cave was probably the first lean-to or shelter in this country. Of course, overhanging cliffs are not always found where we wish to make our camp, so we must resort to other forms of shelter and the use of other materials in such localities.

183

Figure 64

184

A FALLEN-TREE SHELTER

Now that you know how to make a bed in a half cave, we will take up the most simple and primitive manufactured shelters. For a one-night shelter for one man, select a thick-foliaged fir tree and cut it partly through the trunk so it will fall as shown in Figure 65, #11. Trim off the branches on the underside so as to leave room to make your bed beneath the branches. Next trim the branches off the top or roof of the trunk and with them thatch the roof. Do this by setting the branches with their butts up as shown in the right-hand shelter of #13, and then thatch with smaller browse as described in making the bed. This will make a cozy one-night shelter.

If you do not have a tree to cut down, you can create the same effect by following these instructions and taking note of the illustrations: Take three forked sticks (Figure 65, #12), and interlock the forked ends so that they will stand as shown. Over this framework lay a number of poles as shown, or rest branches with the butt ends up as in #13, and thatch this with browse as illustrated by #13. Or take elm, spruce, or birch bark and shingle as in #14. These shelters may be built for one boy, or they may be made large enough for several men. They may be thatched with balsam, spruce, pine, or hemlock boughs, or with cattails, rushes, or any kind of long-stemmed weeds or palmetto leaves.

Of course, common sense and sufficient love of the woods will prevent you from killing or marring and disfiguring trees where trees are not plentiful, and this restriction includes all settled or partially settled parts of the country. Government land carries tree cutting restrictions, and obviously tree cutting on private land is out of the question. It would seem the above method of making your own frame would be best.

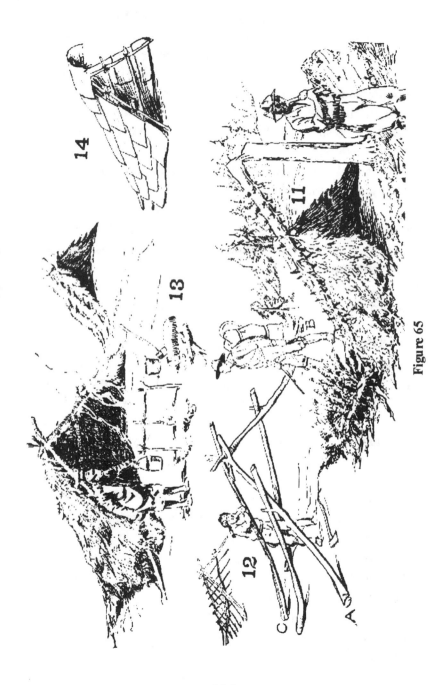

Figure 65

To get birch bark for shingles, select a tree with a smooth trunk devoid of branches and, placing skids for the trunk to fall upon, fell the tree. Then cut a circle around the trunk at the two ends of the log and a slit from one circle clean up to the other circle; next, with a sharp stick shaped like a blunt-edged chisel, pry off the bark carefully until you take the piece off in one whole section. If it is spruce bark or any other bark you seek, hunt through the woods for a comparatively smooth trunk and proceed in the same manner as with the birch.

To take bark off a standing tree, cut one circle down at the butt and another as high as you can reach, and slit it along a perpendicular line connecting the two cuts. This will doubtless in time kill the tree, but far from human habitations the few trees killed in this manner may do the forest good by giving more room for others to grow. Near town or where the forests are small use the bark from the old dead trees.

To shingle with bark, cut the bark in convenient sections, begin at the bottom, place one piece of bark set on edge flat against the wall of your shelter, place a piece of bark next to it in the same manner, allowing the one edge to overlap the first piece a few inches, and so on all the way around your shack; then place a layer of bark above this in the same manner as the first one, the end edges overlapping, the bottom edges also overlapping the first row three or four inches or even more. Hold these pieces of bark in place by stakes driven in the ground against them or poles laid over them, according to the shape or form of your shelter. Continue this way to the comb of the roof. Then over the part where the bark of each side meets on the top, lay another layer of bark covering the crown, ridge, comb, or apex and protecting it from the rain. In the wigwam-shaped shelters, the point of the cone or pyramid is left open to serve as a chimney for smoke to escape.

HOW TO CUT AND NOTCH LOGS

Boys, you have now passed through the grammar school of shack making, you are older than you were when you began, you have acquired more skill and more muscle, and it is time to begin to handle the woodsman's axe, to handle it skillfully and to use it as a tool with which to fashion anything from a table to a two-story house. None of you is too young to learn to use the axe. General Grant, George Washington, Abraham Lincoln, Billy Sunday, all of them could wield an axe by the time they were eight or nine years old and do it without chopping off their toes or splitting any one's head open. We must now get down to the serious work of preparing the logs in order to build us a little cabin of our own, a log clubhouse, or a log camp for hunting.

NOTCHING LOGS

To make the logs hold together at the corners of our cabins it is necessary to lock them in some manner, and the usual way is to notch them. You may cut flat notches like those shown in Figure 66 (A), and this will hold the logs together, as shown by (B). Another way is to flatten only the ends, making the General Putnam joint shown by (C). This joint is named after General Putnam because the log cabins at his old camp near Redding, Connecticut, are made in this manner. Or you may use the Pike notch, which has a wedge-shaped cut on the lower log, made to fit into a triangular notch cut in the upper log, as shown by (D). When fitted together these logs look like the sketch marked (E), which was drawn from a cabin built in this manner.

The simplest notch is the rounded one shown by (F). When these logs are locked together they will fit like those shown by (G).

In the North, the common style of notching logs is to dovetail the ends of the logs (H) so their ends fit snugly together and are also securely locked by their dovetail shape. To build a log house, place the two sill logs on the ground or on the foundation made for them, then two other logs across them, as shown by (I).

HANDLING LOGS

That the logs may be more easily handled, they should be piled up on a skidway which is made by resting the top ends of a number of poles upon a big log or some other sort of elevation and their lower ends upon the ground. With this arrangement the logs may be rolled off without much trouble as they are used, as shown by (J).

CHINKING

A log cabin built with hardwood logs or with pitch-pine logs can seldom be made as tight as one built with the straight spruce logs of the virgin forests. The latter will lie as close as the ones shown by (B), while the former, on account of their unevenness, will have large cracks between them like those shown in (G). These cracks may be filled by quartering small pieces of timber (K) and fitting these quartered pieces into the cracks between the logs where they are held by spikes. This is called "chinking the cabin." To keep the cold and wind out, the cracks may be "mudded up" on the inside with clay or ordinary lime mortar.

MODELS

Study these diagrams carefully, then sit down on the ground with a pile of little sticks alongside you and a sharp jackknife in your hand, and proceed to experiment by building miniature log cabins. This is the best way to plan a large cabin if you intend to erect one. From your model you can see at a glance just how to divide your cabin up into rooms, where you want to place the fireplace, windows, and doors. Always make a small scale model before building.

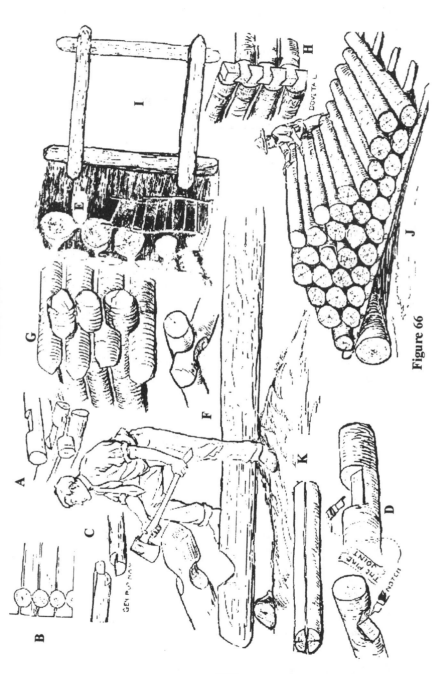

Figure 66

NOTCHED LOG LADDERS

Ever since man learned to use edged tools he has made ladders or steps, by notching logs. A few years ago I took a splendid trip among the Indian cliff dwellings of New Mexico's past generations. My family and I walked trails that had not been changed by man since canoes were invented. There were no roads, no houses, no fences, and no dogs except coyotes. The Indians had long since gone. We were able to climb into some of the cliff dwellings on notched logs ladders, as shown in Figure 67. Our pioneer ancestors used notched log ladders in many ways (see Figure 68). I felt you ought to learn how to make log ladders yourselves.

These are also good ladders to use for tree-houses or even for underground dwellings. Because you have learned how to use the axe, you may make one of these primitive ladders to reach the hayloft in your barn, if you have a barn. You can make the ladder with one log if you set the pole or log upright and notch it on both sides so you can clasp it with your hand and, placing one foot on each side of it, climb up in that manner.

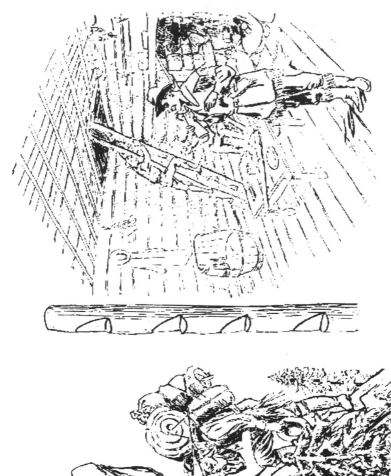

Figure 68

Figure 67

THE LITTLE BEAR OUTDOOR ETHIC

As I conclude, I would like to give you my opinion of the responsible attitude toward animals. I've done quite a lot of thinking about the cleverness of the wild animals, how they live and protect themselves against their enemy. It seems pretty tough on the animals to call man their enemy, but it's close to the truth. There's hardly a four-footed creature or a bird or a fish which doesn't have to keep a wary eye out to see that it isn't killed by the man with the gun.

Of course we do protect the songbirds, but think of the wild fowl that are shot every year. We don't bother the soft-fleshed little minnows, or the spiny sunfish very much, but every trout and salmon and bass has to be sure it isn't making a mistake when it grabs for a fly or a worm. If it isn't careful, it'll soon be browning in the frying pan. We let the field mouse and chipmunk store their food supplies unmolested, but the rabbit, the fox, the deer, and the bear watch and listen and sniff the air for man.

Also there's scarcely a living bird, fish, or four-footed creature that doesn't have to keep its head turned over its shoulder to guard against its "natural" enemies. The kingfisher swoops down on the minnow, the fox pounces on the rabbit, the weasel sucks the warm blood of the fledgling sparrow, the hawk takes the partridge, the lynx kills the fawn. It's an eternal fight to escape, and that is the way of nature.

Some sentimental people have tried to make us believe that the wild animals of the forest live in continual fear and unhappiness, but that's not true. All those animals take it pretty much as a matter of course. They watch out for danger just the way we watch out not to get hit by an automobile when we cross the street. They look and listen and scent the breeze automatically, ever on the alert, and it's all in the day's work and play. If you've seen a bird escape by

193

a hairsbreadth from the spread claws of a cat, you've probably noticed that almost the next moment the bird is going about its singing and worm hunting as unconcerned as ever.

Here's what I think the true sportsman's attitude should be toward the creatures of the woods and waters: Never kill anything just for the fun of it. These animals and birds and fishes fulfill a purpose on this earth. Most of them are useful, and all of them are interesting. Get to know them. Learn the secrets of their lives. If you take a fish for your frying pan or bring down a duck for your campfire meal, do it with thankfulness to the Lord who provides for all our needs.

Life is precious, and it is a gift from God who created all things for His purposes, and our delight. We have a responsibility over the creation He created, and we will be held accountable for our stewardship. Game animals are healthful to eat and are placed on earth for our dominion over them. All food should be received with thanksgiving to God. Someday, according to the Bible, the lion and the lamb will lie down together, and the animal kingdom will be at peace with one another, and with mankind. Until then, if you are a hunter, respect the life of the creature, appreciate it, and kill only what you will use wisely.

In His Providential Care
"Little Bear" Wheeler

Resource Guide for Various Materials

1. For steel traps, calls, and lures write
PACIFIC HIDE and FUR DEPOT
P.O. BOX 3324
Spokane, WA 99220
Call: 509-535-1673
List of trapping supplies available
E-mail pacificspk@sina.com

2. For a place to buy and sell hides and antlers, contact:
MOSCOW HIDE and FUR
P.O. BOX 8918
Moscow, ID 83843
208-882-0601
Catalog on the web: www.furbuyer.com

3. Looking for real Indian tipis and other primitive shelters
with all the primitive camping items?
Write or call for a free catalog:
PANTHER PRIMITIVES
P.O. BOX 32
Normantown, WV 25267
304-462-7718

4. Want to play cowboy dress up for real? **TEXAS JACK'S**
has clothing guns, and other items from the period of 1860-
1887 everything to look like Roy Rodgers or Dale Evens.
TEXAS JACK'S
117 North Adams St
Fredricksburg, TX 78624
Call: 1-800-TEX-JACKS
Catalog on the web: www.texasjacks.com

5. If buying period clothing is too expensive, then this is the source for you. **Amazon Drygoods** has a catalog of period patterns for you to sew, even coonskin hat patterns. Request the pattern catalog.

AMAZONE DRYGOODS
2218 East 11th St.
Davenport, IA 52803
Call: 319-322-6800

6. Want to play Indian dress up for real? **CRAZY CROW TRADING POST** has arrowheads, Indian beads, feathers, headdresses, bear claws, and all you need to play Tonto and the Lone Ranger.
Write: **CRAZY CROWS TRADING POST**
P.O. BOX 847
Pottsboro, TX 75076
1-800-786-6210
Catalog on the web: www.crazycrow.com

7. Want to make your own Davy Crockett rifle, or throw a knife and tomahawk? How about starting a flint and steel fire? **DIXIE GUN WORKS** has everything you can imagine for the family who wants to step back into the 1700s to 1880s.
Write: **DIXIE GUN WORKS INC.**
P.O. BOX 130
Union City, TN 38261
1-800-238-6785
Catalog on the web: www.dixiegun.com

8. If Dixie Gun Works is too expensive and you want authentic-looking non-firing guns and rifles, **COLLECTOR'S ARMOURY** is the place for your budget.
COLLECTOR'S ARMOURY
P.O. BOX 59, Dept. 20-I
Alexandria, VA 22313-0059
Call: 1-800-599-9994
Catalog on the web: www.collectorsarmoury.com

9. For many of my American Revolution and colonial items I have used **JAS. TOWNSEND & SON, INC.** Items for the whole family are available. It is worth getting their catalog and looking over their materials.
JAS. TOWNSEND & SON, INC.
P.O. BOX 415
Pierceton, IN 46562
Call: 1-800-338-1665
Catalog on the web: www.jastown.com

10. My dear friends at Vision Forum have put together the neatest men and boys catalog called *THE ALL-AMERICAN BOY'S ADVENTURE CATALOG.* The catalog is divided into themes: Tools for Boys, Early American Boyhood, Little Bear's Hero Page, Boy's Adventure Library, Pioneers & Pilgrims of the Old West, and lots more. *(Tell them Little Bear sent you, and postage will be free of charge.)*
Write: **VISION FORUM**
32335 U.S. Hwy. 281 North
Bulverde, TX 78163-3158
Call: 1-888-322-8718
Catalog on the web: visionforum.com

11. Yours truly, **MANTLE MINISTRIES.** Many people do not realize that our ministry has produced some wonderful outdoor adventure videos in which I dress up and tell historical stories. I have devotional historical cassettes from the 1600s to the 1880s. We have also republished lost and forgotten classic books on the Old West called *The Old West Series.* For a catalog and listing of our products, write:

MANTLE MINISTRIES
228 Still Ridge
Bulverde, TX 78163
Call: Toll Free 1-877-LIT-BEAR (548-2327)
Catalog on the web: www.mantlemin.com
E-mail: mantleministries@cs.com

If you are interested in reading the fascinating autobiography of "Little Bear" Wheeler, write: Mantle Ministries at the above address.

Special offer: *The "Little Bear" Story* normally sells for $8.00. Having purchased *The "Little Bear's" Outdoor Adventure Guide* allows you this special price of $6.00 each.